One Devoted Man

One Devoted Man

D.L. Moody

Nancy Drummond

CF4·K

10 9 8 7 6 5 4 3 2 1

Copyright © Nancy Drummond 2015

Paperback ISBN: 978-1-78191-676-6

epub ISBN: 978-1-78191-670-4

mobi ISBN: 978-1-78191-671-1

Published by
Christian Focus Publications,
Geanies House, Fearn, Tain, Ross-shire,
IV20 1TW, Scotland, U.K.
Tel: 01862 871011
Fax: 01862 871699
www.christianfocus.com
email: info@christianfocus.com

Cover design by Daniel van Straaten
Cover illustration by Jeff Anderson
American English is used throughout this book
Printed and bound in Denmark by Nørhaven

Scripture quotations are taken from
the King James Version of the Bible.

This book is written in a conversational style. Its use of dialogue
is fictional, but used in such a way as to get across facts and
history with a relaxed and easily read approach.

Contents

The First Decade

The round-faced, pudgy-kneed boy barely noticed the sunlight beating down on his dark brown hair as he intently studied the approaching stagecoach. As it rumbled closer, Dwight fingered the money in his pocket. When he could taste the dust in the air and hear the horses breathing heavily, he waved his arms wildly. The stagecoach stopped a few feet up the road, and Dwight ran to the driver's box.

"Can I help you, young man?" the driver asked kindly.

"I need a ride to my grandmother's house, please, sir," Dwight answered.

"Do you have money for the fare?"

Dwight pulled his money out and held it out, squinting up at the driver.

"I'm sorry," the driver said, shaking his head. "The fare is ten cents, and you only have five cents there. If my stagecoach was empty, I might consider it. But as you can see..."

The driver waved his arm at the crowded stage, and Dwight's small shoulders slumped. It was a sweaty, exhausting, four-mile walk to Grandmother Holton's house. He chewed his lip in concentration. Then he gave an excited hop.

"Would five cents buy me a seat on top?"

Giggles rippled through the passenger compartment, and the driver looked down at Dwight.

"I beg your pardon, young man—what do you mean 'on top'?"

Dwight pointed to the luggage on the roof of the stagecoach, and said, "Up there—with the bags, sir."

There were more giggles as the driver tipped his head and considered Dwight's proposal. Dwight shifted his weight from foot to foot and looked down at the dusty road. It was the longest few seconds of his five-year-old life! Finally, the driver smiled down at him.

"I suppose five cents could buy you a seat up there," he said, pulling Dwight up and settling him among the bags and boxes. "Welcome aboard…and hang on!"

After a day with Grandmother Holton and his cousins, aunts, and uncles, Dwight had spent time formulating a plan for the trip home. His cousins urged him to head home early so he would reach the house safely before dark. But Dwight dawdled on the road, armed with a bushy bouquet of wildflowers and caraway. When he heard the familiar rumble of the stagecoach headed toward him, Dwight smiled his best smile.

When Dwight waved his arms, the driver pulled over. He looked down and rolled his eyes.

"You again! Do you have the fare this time young man?"

Dwight smiled widely and held his bouquet high. The driver laughed and shook his head.

"I should have known," he muttered, chuckling softly. "The luggage rack again?"

"Yes, please, sir," Dwight answered.

The driver hoisted him up to the roof of the stagecoach and patted Dwight's head fondly, saying, "You are a very persuasive young man!"

Persuasion was always one of Dwight's greatest resources. Born February 5th, 1837, as the sixth of nine children with a widowed mother, Dwight's young life sometimes felt like a struggle to survive. Before his father died, things had been fairly normal and routine, with a sense of comfort and plenty. But when Dwight was just four years old, his father died unexpectedly. Then the twins were born, the debt collectors came, and everything turned upside down.

Edwin Moody, Dwight's father, was deep in debt when he died, and he left no money to pay what he owed. The creditors took everything but the house, which was protected by law. Dwight's mother, Betsy, had just had twins, and found herself without food or supplies for her large family. The creditors even took the kindling for the fire.

Betsy's family immediately came to her aid. Dwight woke up one frosty morning to the chop-chop-chop of Uncle Cyrus cutting wood. He worked for hours, making sure there was plenty of wood to get Betsy and her children through the long, cold New England winter. As the midmorning sun began to warm the landscape, Dwight slipped outside and watched Uncle Cyrus chopping tirelessly

"Why are you chopping wood for us?" Dwight asked.

Uncle Cyrus stopped working and mopped his brow with his jacket sleeve. "Because I love you. And because you have a need. When you love people, you take care of them."

Dwight turned that idea over and over in his little head as Uncle Cyrus returned to his chopping. It was a new concept, but it was one Dwight would never forget. Just like Uncle Cyrus, a local minister helped reinforce the lesson by providing food and clothes for the Moody family that summer and enrolling the older children in Sunday School.

In the Moody household, church attendance was not optional on Sundays, and they always dressed their best. In fact, Dwight and the other boys walked to church barefoot to keep their shoes clean. When they were within sight of the church, the boys would stop and slip on their socks and shoes. Then they walked into church, clean and tidy.

As Dwight grew older, he learned to put on a good show. Although he occasionally fell asleep during services—and once even had the preacher send a messenger to wake him up!—Dwight was generally the picture of good behavior. He was angelic when his mother was around, but when Mrs. Moody wasn't watching, Dwight was constantly looking for opportunities for mischief.

One winter day, Dwight gathered a group of boys after school. Several of them squeezed into a box-shaped toboggan and rode it down a steep hill, right behind Old Man Squires' house. The speed of the toboggan as it crashed through a fence, coupled with the boys' raucous laughter, terrified the old man's cattle. They stampeded through fences and trampled fields. Dwight and the other boys abandoned the toboggan and pretended to be just as shocked and indignant as everyone else.

Another cold, dreary day, Dwight posted a fake notice on the schoolhouse door about a guest speaker who was coming to town. On the night listed on the notice, the schoolhouse was lit and warmed, and most of the town showed up. The time for the meeting came and went. Soon, the people began to grumble, and Dwight—who had seated himself in the middle of the crowd—grumbled louder than anyone. Of course, the fictional speaker never showed up, and only Dwight knew why!

It was a carefree life, and Dwight was determined to enjoy every minute of it. But he was almost ten years old, and everything was about to change.

The Journey to Independence

Dwight had done odd jobs around town since he was a small boy, but when he turned ten, it was time for him to get a real job. He traveled to a town thirteen miles from his home to work for people he had never met. As he walked down the main street of the town, his eyes darting from the weathered storefronts to the unfamiliar faces, an old man touched his arm. Dwight jumped.

"Are you new in town, boy?"

"Yes, sir. It's my first day here," Dwight admitted, his voice barely above a whisper.

"And who is your father? Perhaps I have heard of him."

"My father was Edwin Moody of Northfield," Dwight answered. "But he passed away when I was just a small boy."

The old man smiled kindly. "And you are a small boy still," he said, gently squeezing Dwight's arm. "Although you have no earthly father, you have a Heavenly Father who loves you very much. Do you know that, young man?"

Dwight nodded. He could not pull his gaze away from the warm twinkle of the old man's pale blue eyes.

"Good boy!" the old man exclaimed. "Never forget how much your Heavenly Father loves you." He paused. "May I pray a blessing over you?"

"Yes, sir," Dwight said, bowing his head and squeezing his eyes shut.

The old man placed a bony, broad hand on Dwight's head and prayed a blessing over him, his work, and his future. Then he gave Dwight a shiny coin and said goodbye.

Dwight put the coin in his pocket and hurried to his new job. As he scurried down the crowded street, he could still feel the warmth of the old man's hand on his head. It was a sweet feeling that seeped from his head down into his heart. Throughout those lonely first weeks away from home, Dwight often pulled out the coin and fingered its smooth, cool surface. And every time he pulled it out, he felt the balm of love and acceptance soothe his soul.

It didn't take Dwight long to fall into the routine of working away from home. It was not so different than going to school, but there was more variety and more independence. Dwight liked the people he worked for, and he soon made friends in town. He was secretly glad his classroom days were over.

When a short-term job ended, Dwight would return home until the next job opened up. This pattern of home-away-home-away continued until Dwight was seventeen. Then he decided he was ready to leave home for good to seek his path in life.

"Are you sure you're ready for Boston, Dwight?" Mrs. Moody asked.

"Yes, Mother," Dwight assured her. "It's high time for me to make a living on my own. I am a man, not a boy anymore."

Mrs. Moody took Dwight's face in her hands. There were tears in her eyes, but her smile was wide and warm.

"Just remember," she told him, "you will always have a place here at home."

With only five dollars to his name, Dwight climbed aboard a stagecoach bound for Boston. He was determined to make his way in the "big city" without any help from anyone. He had two uncles in the shoe business, but Dwight didn't want help from family or anyone else.

For a few weeks, Dwight stayed anywhere he could find a room and did whatever odd jobs came his way. He scoured the city for regular work, but no one seemed willing to hire a country boy with no references. Finally, in desperation, Dwight went to his uncle's shoe store.

Samuel Holton, Betsy Moody's brother, was a well-known and respected businessman in Boston. His sister had written to tell him Dwight was coming to town, and he smiled to himself as Dwight walked through his shop door. Samuel had been expecting this visit.

"Dwight!" Samuel exclaimed, crossing the room to shake his nephew's hand. "It's good to see you, my boy. How have you been?"

Dwight stood as tall and straight as he could and tried to sound distinguished. "I'm well, thank you." He took a deep breath and blurted, "Uncle Samuel, I have come to ask you for a job."

Samuel tried to sound surprised. "A job? Dwight, I'm not sure there is a good place for you here."

"Uncle Samuel, I'm a hard worker. And I learn new things quickly. I know I could do well in your store."

Samuel sensed the desperation edging into his nephew's voice. He rubbed his chin thoughtfully. Dwight squirmed anxiously under his uncle's piercing stare.

"Dwight," Samuel said finally, "I am afraid if you come in here you will want to run the store yourself. Now, my men here want to do their work the way I want it done. Do you think you can do that?"

Dwight's tense face relaxed into a grin. "Oh yes, Uncle Samuel! I can do that."

"I want you to promise to do your best," Samuel continued. "And I want you to promise to do your work right, with no shortcuts. And ask questions when you don't know the answers."

"I will. I promise."

Samuel put his hands on Dwight's shoulders and looked right into his eyes.

"Dwight, you must also promise that you will attend Sunday School every week and live a clean life. Are you willing to commit to that?"

"Yes, sir," Dwight answered sincerely.

"Then you have a job!"

Within a few short weeks, Dwight had learned the ropes of being a shoe salesman. Before long, he was the best salesman Samuel's store had ever seen. Dwight was working hard, just like he promised. And he was keeping his other promises too, living right and faithfully going to church and Sunday School at Mount Vernon Congregational Church.

Dwight's Sunday School teacher was Edward Kimball, who took a personal interest in all his students. He soon noticed Dwight was religious, but didn't have a personal relationship with God. Mr. Kimball prayed about the right time to talk to Dwight about asking Jesus to be his personal Savior.

One day, Mr. Kimball just knew the time was finally right. He headed down to Samuel Holton's shoe store and approached a salesman.

"Excuse me," Mr. Kimball said, "I'm looking for Dwight Moody. Can you please tell me where to find him?"

The salesman took Mr. Kimball to the back room and pointed toward the corner. "He's over there."

Dwight looked up from the shoes he was wrapping and grinned broadly.

"Mr. Kimball!" he exclaimed, stepping forward to shake his teacher's outstretched hand. "What a nice surprise! What brings you here?"

"Dwight, it's time you and I had a talk."

They sat on benches in the back room of the store, and Mr. Kimball told Dwight the old, familiar story of Jesus coming to earth to die in the place of sinners, to save them from the punishment they deserved for their sins.

"Do you believe God loves you, Dwight?" Mr Kimball asked.

"Well, yes, Mr. Kimball."

"In Romans 10:9-10 the Bible tells us that, if we confess our faith in Jesus with our mouths and believe in Him in our hearts, we will be saved." Mr. Kimball studied Dwight's face, and then he went on. "Are you ready to do that today, Dwight? Are ready to make God the head of your life?"

Dwight looked at the floor for a moment. Then he nodded. Together, Dwight and Mr. Kimball bowed their heads and Dwight poured his heart out to God. He apologized for the wrong choices he had made. He thanked God for His overwhelming love. And he promised to serve God and spend his life as a representative of his Heavenly Father.

From the doorway, Dwight's uncle Samuel watched with tears of joy in his eyes. He knew this would be a turning point in Dwight's life. But even he could not have imagined how much of a turning point it would be.

When they finished praying, Mr. Kimball put his hand on Dwight's shoulder and said, "This is a new beginning for you, Dwight. Before, you were a good man. Now, through God, you can be a truly great man. I can hardly wait to see what greatness God will accomplish in your life!"

The energy Dwight had devoted toward being a great salesman was now focused on being a light for Christ. He still excelled at his job, but now Dwight's life had new purpose. He shared his heart with Mr. Kimball when the teacher stopped by the shoe store again a few weeks later.

"I'm seventeen years old," Dwight said, "and I feel like I have already wasted so much time. Before my conversion, I worked toward the cross, but since then I have worked from the cross; then I worked to be saved, but now I work because I am saved."

Mr. Kimball beamed. "You are on the right path, Dwight. Keep walking in Christ, and take it one day at a time. He will bless you, and when you trust Him, he will take you further than you could ever dream possible."

Dwight was happier than he had ever been, and he was filled with a greater zeal and energy than he had ever known. But over the next two years, a desire to do more grew in Dwight's soul. Finally, he knew he could not stay in Boston any more.

A Western Adventure

On an impulse, Dwight decided Chicago was where he belonged. One of America's westernmost large cities at that time, Chicago was considered a blend of untamed frontier and urban opportunity. Dwight was sure Chicago was where he would find his fortune and his future.

Without a word to his family, Dwight packed his meager belongings and moved over 1,000 miles—halfway across the country—to make his mark on the city of Chicago. On September 25th, 1856, not long after he arrived, Dwight sent a letter to his mother.

"I reached this far-famed city of the West one week ago tonight," he wrote. "I went into a prayer meeting last night, and as soon as I made myself known, I had friends enough."

Later in the letter, he added, "God is the same here as He was in Boston, and in Him I can find peace."

Within two days of his arrival in Chicago, Dwight had found work as a shoe salesman. He was even more successful in his new city than he had been in Boston.

There was greater opportunity in Chicago, and Dwight soon made a name for himself. He began traveling for his bosses, selling shoes to smaller stores throughout the Midwest.

Despite his success in the business world, Dwight never forgot that God was the source of his blessings. Soon after his arrival in Chicago, Dwight joined Plymouth Church. To help raise funds, the church rented pews to the congregation. A person would rent a pew and then bring friends and neighbors to fill it. This concept was a personal challenge to Dwight.

Thinking back to his schoolboy days when he would often drag his friends to Sunday School with him, Dwight decided he would surpass his old records. He rented a pew and soon filled it with acquaintances, friends, and even occasional strangers. Within weeks, Dwight's single rented pew had become four rented pews, and they were filled to capacity every Sunday.

During the week, as he was scouting out new prospects as a shoe salesman, he was also scouting out new prospects for his Sunday pews! For business, Dwight spent time in hotels and train depots. But for Sunday School, he looked where other Christians often refused to look: poor boarding houses, street corners in crime-ridden neighborhoods, and even saloons.

Dwight took the words of Jesus in Luke 14:23 very seriously. Jesus said, "Go out into the highways and hedges, and compel them to come in, that my house may be filled." Dwight was determined to do just that.

He saw the poor and rejected souls of Chicago as his mission field, because he remembered well what it felt like to be poor and rejected.

In January 1857, Dwight wrote to his mother and said, "I go to meeting every night. Oh, how I do enjoy it! It seems as if God was here Himself. Oh, Mother, pray for us. Pray that this work may go on until every knee is bowed."

Dwight had an endless supply of energy and ideas, and he hated sitting idle. Since his Sunday afternoons and evenings stretched out long and empty, Dwight went out searching for something productive to do with his time. Wandering the streets of Chicago, he found a small mission Sunday School meeting in a building on North Wells Street. Curious, Dwight wandered in and approached a studious man who was straightening long rows of chairs.

"Hello," Dwight said, introducing himself with a warm handshake. "Are you in charge here?"

"I suppose you could say that," the man answered. "I work here, anyway. How can I help you?"

"I was wondering what it is exactly that you do here."

"Well," the man replied, "we run a small Sunday School every Sunday afternoon. It isn't much—we only have about twenty pupils—but we do what we can."

"I am a Christian with an interest in ministering to young people," Dwight said. "How might I go about becoming a teacher in your Sunday School?"

The man sighed. "I wish I had a class to offer you. But right now, we have more teachers than students."

Dwight was surprised. "What are you doing to recruit more students? There must be many children in this neighborhood."

"There are many children," the man agreed. "But none of us have the time and energy to chase them down. We pray they will come, and we encourage those who do come to bring their friends."

He looked away and went back to straightening the chairs. His shoulders slumped a little, and there was a general hopelessness about him. Dwight sensed a big challenge in the little Sunday School, and he was never one for backing down from a challenge.

"What if I created my own class?"

The man looked up. "What do you mean?"

"Well," Dwight said, "if I bring my own pupils, can I teach a class?"

The man considered this for a moment. "I don't see why not. If you create your own class, I suppose we can find a place for you to teach."

Dwight grinned. "See you next Sunday then."

Although he didn't consider himself much of a teacher, Dwight was determined to build a class. He was great at talking to people—it was exactly what made him a good salesman—and he could convince people of almost anything. Throughout the week, Dwight hung around the streets and alleys surrounding the North Wells Street Sunday School, making friends, talking to people, and getting to know the community.

When Sunday afternoon came, Dwight walked into the Sunday School building with eighteen little pupils trailing behind him. In a single week, he had almost doubled the attendance of the mission Sunday School! Heads turned to stare as Dwight led the ragged little procession to their seats. The children were short and tall, lanky teenagers and pudgy little boys, all dressed in mismatched suits with faded stains and elbow patches. To the rest of the Sunday School, they were "hoodlums", but to Dwight, they were his class, and he loved them already.

Every Sunday, Dwight brought more pupils and new faces. It wasn't long before the North Wells Street Sunday School outgrew their small space and moved to a larger building. Other teachers caught Dwight's passion and spirit, and many of them began seeking out and bringing in pupils of their own.

After nearly two years at the North Wells Street Sunday School, Dwight decided to start a new mission Sunday School in another part of Chicago. In the fall of 1858, he went looking for a building large enough to accommodate his vision. After an extensive search, Dwight found North Market Hall, a large space above a popular city market.

The building was a huge brick edifice, crumbling in places due to age and neglect. Inside and up a long set of creaky stairs was the great hall. It was wallpapered with several layers of grime and filth, a bare, dingy cavern of a room. But when Dwight looked at it, he saw potential.

"I would like to rent the North Market Hall every Sunday for a year—and maybe longer," Dwight announced when he contacted the owner.

"That can be arranged," the owner replied. "But you should know that a German Society holds a dance in the hall on Saturday nights. And they are no good at cleaning up after themselves."

Dwight shrugged. "I'm sure it's nothing I haven't had to deal with before."

A price was negotiated, a deal was struck, and Dwight began a new Sunday ritual. Every Sunday morning, he was up by 6:00 a.m., hurrying down to North Market Hall. He would roll away the empty beer kegs and sweep up the thick layer of sawdust from the floor. Then Dwight would give the mammoth room a general cleaning and carefully arrange hundreds of chairs for the Sunday School students. It was hard work, and lonely, since he did it all himself. However, Dwight didn't mind.

When all the work was done and the hall was ready, Dwight wandered through the community, reminding children and parents alike that Sunday School would soon be starting. Children would join Dwight along the way, so when he arrived back at North Market Hall, his lonely pilgrimage had become a large procession.

Sunday School began at 2:00 p.m., and the hall was often filled with 500 to 600 rowdy street children.

The air was ripe with mischief and fun, but when the lesson began, a blanket of silence fell over the group, and even the wiggles and whispers ceased. After the service, Dwight stood at the door, greeting hundreds of boys and girls with smiles, handshakes, and personal words of encouragement.

When Sunday School was finally over, Dwight still wasn't ready to rest! He hurried through the neighborhoods, visiting absentees and inviting everyone he met to come to the evening service. Dwight led the evening service, and then he stayed after the service to talk with those who needed special prayer. It was a crazy, chaotic, exhausting, exhilarating routine, and Dwight happily repeated it week after week after week.

Dwight's love for people and commitment to the mission did not go unnoticed. Soon the Sunday School grew to more than 1,500 students, and evening services were held nearly every night of the week. People came from all denominations and all levels of society. They were enchanted and inspired by Dwight's genuine passion.

But not everyone loved Dwight. After one of the evening services for adults, a man approached Dwight.

"Thank you for coming tonight," Dwight said warmly, extending his hand.

The man shook Dwight's outstretched hand half-heartedly and said, "You make too many mistakes in grammar."

Without missing a beat, Dwight responded, "I know I make mistakes, and I lack a great many things, but I'm doing the best I can with what I've got."

Dwight paused and studied the man, who squirmed uncomfortably under the direct gaze. Finally, Dwight spoke again.

"Look here, friend," he encouraged, "you've got grammar enough—what are you doing with it for the Master?"

The man hurried away, but his stinging remarks had sparked an idea in Dwight's mind. It would mean some changes in the popular Sunday School routine, but Dwight was sure it would put things even more on the right track.

Perspective Changes
Everything

Dwight began delegating more and more of the Sunday School responsibilities to others. He realized his lack of education could be a detriment to the ministry, and he wanted God's mission to succeed to the fullest. He asked a few local businessmen to be superintendents and help balance the administrative duties. Dwight also assigned pupils to teachers with the understanding that they could switch teachers whenever they liked so they could find a teacher whose teaching style matched the way they learned. The underlying spirit of competition this created motivated all of the teachers to do their best.

Although by later 1858, Dwight was head of the largest Sunday School in the United States, he was also the most eager pupil, sitting in classes and drinking in information. At the same time, he was also still working hard as a shoe salesman, traveling frequently throughout the week. He loved being busy, but he was so busy he was losing sight of his ultimate goals.

"I'm facing a difficult decision," Dwight confided to a close friend as they walked through a neighborhood one chilly afternoon.

"What decision is that?"

Dwight studied the children skipping by, chasing stray dogs and playing stickball in the narrow streets. Many of them stopped to wave at Dwight.

"I have never lost sight of Jesus Christ since the first time I met Him in the store in Boston," Dwight admitted. "But for years I have really believed that I could not work for God. And now I find myself being called to do just that. What I must decide is whether or not now is the right time to abandon my career as a salesman and devote myself fully to God's work."

While Dwight was still struggling with this decision, one of his Sunday School teachers became terminally ill. He knew he would be dying soon, and he wanted to spend his last weeks with his family in New York. But before he left, something was heavy on his heart. He took his concerns to Dwight.

"Mr. Moody," he began, his voice weak from his illness, "I have loved my students and encouraged them to learn and attend Sunday School faithfully, but I have never personally led a single one of them to salvation in Jesus."

Dwight thought about the teacher's large class of older girls. They were a wild bunch, causing trouble in the community, disrupting church services, mocking the teachers and preachers, and antagonizing everyone in authority. The humble teacher had been tireless and patient in his work with these girls, but none of them had experienced God's transformative power in their lives. With a sudden pang of guilt and regret, Dwight realized the Sunday School was too often about numbers—bringing people in the doors rather than bringing them to Jesus.

"How can I help, my friend?" Dwight asked.

"I want to visit each one of my girls before I leave next week," the teacher insisted. "I can't leave in peace unless I clearly give each one the chance to accept Jesus as their personal Savior."

"Are you sure you are strong enough?"

"I believe God will give me the strength I need to carry out this one last mission," the teacher said. "Remember what Paul wrote—when I am weak, God is strong in me."

"I will hire a carriage and come with you," Dwight offered.

"Oh, Mr. Moody, I can't ask you to do that! You are a busy man with many important things to do. Just help me get a carriage, if you will. This is my work, and I'll be fine."

Dwight was insistent. "God's work and your work are my work, too. I will come with you."

The next morning, Dwight and the teacher headed out in the bright sunlight. They came to the first house on the list, where they were invited inside. As his eyes adjusted to the dim little shack, Dwight instantly recognized the girl sitting sullenly on a chair in the furthest corner of the room. She was the worst of all the troublemakers in the class.

Without hesitation, the teacher crossed the dirty, cluttered room and took a seat beside the girl. Dwight followed him.

"Mary," the teacher began softly. The girl glanced at him, and then looked the other way.

"Mary," he began again, more assertively this time. "I'm dying. The doctors say I only have a few more weeks to live."

Momentary shock played across the girl's face, but then her expression settled back into hard lines of defiance. She studied the floor.

"I'm going away in a few days," the teacher continued. "I'm going to spend some time with my family in New York. And after that, I'll be going on to Heaven. I know that, because I have trusted in Jesus as my Savior."

He paused, and Mary looked up and met his steady gaze.

"Mary, I want you to go to Heaven someday, too. You know that I care for you, but Jesus loves you—more than I ever could. He loves you so much that He died for you."

Mary was listening now. The lines on her face had softened, and her eyes studied her teacher's face.

"How could He love me?" she asked, a hint of sorrowful disbelief in her voice. "No one loves me. I'm mean and stupid and ugly and worthless."

Mary bit her lip and swallowed hard. The teacher put a hand on her shoulder.

"Jesus wants you to have your sins forgiven and give you a whole new life. Do you want that, Mary?"

She nodded, swiping at the tears that spilled onto her cheeks. "I want a new life," she whispered with a half sob. "But are you sure Jesus wants a girl like me?"

"I am sure," the teacher said with a gentle smile, blinking back tears of his own. "Mr. Moody, will you pray with her?"

Dwight bowed his head and prayed over Mary. Then he led her to confess her sins and ask Jesus to be the Lord of her life. When the prayer was over, Mary looked up at Dwight. Her eyes shone with a new light, and the angry lines on her face had softened.

"Thank you, Mr. Moody," she said, wiping away her last few tears. Then she turned to her Sunday School teacher and hugged him impulsively. "And how can I ever thank you enough for caring so much about me?"

"My dream is for all of you girls to someday meet me in Heaven," he told her. "And now—for you—that dream is a reality. That is thanks enough for me!"

As they climbed back into the carriage, the teacher turned to Dwight. "That's one," he said, "but there are so many more."

They continued in prayerful silence to the next house on the list, where the whole scene was repeated.

From house to house they went, with the teacher baring his soul to each one of his wayward pupils. After several stops, he looked at Dwight with a pale face and haunted eyes.

"I wish I could continue on my mission," the teacher murmured, "but I don't think I have the strength to make even one more stop."

Dwight patted his shoulder. "My friend," he said, "it is not required of you to try to do what you cannot do. God is not a hard Master. Just as you have expressed His love to these girls, He wants to express His love to you. Go home and rest now. We can go out again tomorrow."

Every day for the next ten days, Dwight and the dedicated teacher visited girls from the class. As they climbed wearily into the carriage on the afternoon of the tenth day, the teacher turned to Dwight with tear-filled eyes.

"That was the last one," he said with a sigh. "They are all on their way to Heaven now. And now, I can go home with peace in my heart."

On impulse, Dwight suggested they call the class together that evening for one last meeting, since the teacher was leaving the next day. Word was sent throughout the neighborhoods, and the girls eagerly agreed to come to the meeting.

Every girl they had visited over their ten-day mission showed up at the meeting that night. They crowded into the room, and the teacher sat before them. Dwight hovered on the outskirts of the gathering, feeling a little like an intruder, but craving the unique joy that filled the room.

"I am leaving you tomorrow," the teacher told them. "But I am leaving you with the full assurance that I will see you all in Heaven someday. And that gives me both peace and hope!"

He read John 14 to the girls and reminded them of their promised home in Heaven. When he had finished, the girls were quiet for a moment. Then Mary jumped up.

"God in Heaven," she prayed aloud, "I ask that you would bless our dear teacher. He cared for our souls, and now we ask that you would care for him. Send your Spirit to comfort his spirit and body, and walk beside him as you now walk beside us."

As soon as Mary took her seat, another girl stood to pray. One by one, every girl in the class spoke a blessing over the teacher who had so richly blessed them. With tattered dresses and uncombed hair, they approached the Creator of the Universe in humble thanks for the one man who had cared enough to tell them about the Almighty God who wanted to be their Eternal Friend.

The next evening, without any prompting, the girls all gathered one last time at the train station to see their teacher off on his final earthly journey. With damp cheeks and a mixture of joy and sadness, the teacher bid them one last goodbye. They waved as he boarded the train and found his seat. As the train pulled away from the station, the teacher made his way back through the train and emerged on the platform of the rear car of the train. Their last glimpse of him was on that platform, pointing toward Heaven, with a glorious smile lighting his face.

Dwight felt a lump rise in his throat as he realized he was witnessing what could happen when one man did his genuine best to live out his faith. As the girls said goodbye to their teacher that night, Dwight said goodbye to his dearly held ambitions for worldly success as a merchant and businessman. He knew what he had to do, and it would take him on a whole new journey of his own.

A Full-time Focus

From that day forward, Dwight decided to give up his business pursuits and give his life fully to ministry. He knew he would have to live off his savings—for the most part, at least—so he adjusted his lifestyle accordingly. He moved out of his comfortable boarding-house into a cramped room at the YMCA. He ate his meals at cheap restaurants and pinched pennies wherever he could.

Having no other career freed Dwight's time to focus on the Sunday School and visiting students. His methods were often unorthodox, but they worked. He visited students in their homes and used those visits to also evangelize their parents. He threw his heart and soul into encouraging his existing pupils and finding new ones, young and old.

One day during his wanderings, Dwight saw a lonely-looking girl in a tattered dress scurrying along the shady side of the street. He hurried to catch up with her.

"Hello, young lady," Dwight said. "How are you today?"

"I'm fine, sir," she said timidly.

"I work in a Sunday School near here, at North Market Hall," Dwight told her. "Would you like to come visit our Sunday School?"

"I would like to hear more about it, sir," she said. "But first I must run an errand. If you will wait right here, I will be back soon."

Dwight leaned against a fence and waited for the little girl to return. Five minutes passed, then ten minutes, and then a half hour. The sun climbed high in the sky as Dwight waited, chatting with the passersby. Finally, after three hours of waiting, Dwight decided the girl was not going to return. He was heartbroken, but he didn't even know where to begin looking for her.

A few days later, Dwight was strolling through a different neighborhood when he caught sight of the little girl. He called out to her, but as her eyes met his, she turned and ran. Dwight, determined not to lose her, followed the girl down broad streets and through narrow alleys. He spotted her turning into a saloon and Dwight raced in after her. The young girl tucked herself away in a favorite hiding spot. Dwight ducked down and peered into the darkness, trying to catch his breath.

"Why did you run?" Dwight panted.

"Go away, please, sir," the girl begged.

"What are you afraid of?"

The girl's pale face emerged from the shadows. "I'm not afraid, sir," she admitted. "I am ashamed."

Dwight took a seat. "Why are you ashamed?"

"When my father died last year, this saloon was all he left us," the little girl admitted, twisting her dress between her fingers. "My mama hates it. She always did say it was the devil's business. But now that it's all we have, she has to run the saloon to put food on the table."

The little girl looked down and sighed. Dwight waited for her to go on.

"Mama is always unhappy now. It makes me sad."

Dwight studied her for a moment. "I'm still not sure why you ran away from me."

"Well," the girl said, fingering her hem again, "if Mama thinks this is the devil's business, I figured you would too. And since you are from a church, I was afraid of what you would think of me when you found out where I lived and who I was."

"Now that I know who you are, do you know what I think?"

The little girl shook her head. Dwight grinned.

"I think I would like you to come to Sunday School, just like I said before."

Dwight went with the little girl and talked with her mother. By the following Sunday, the little girl and her brothers and sisters were all enrolled in Sunday School. Within a few months, Dwight had helped the mother close down the saloon and find another way to provide for her family. He believed in changing lives and transforming situations, because he served a God who was famous for changing lives and transforming situations.

Another night, Dwight was on his way home when he noticed a man leaning listlessly against a lamppost. Dwight walked up to the man and put his hands on the man's shoulders.

"Are you a Christian, friend?" Dwight asked, his eyes searching the man's face.

"I'm not your friend," the man shouted, pushing angrily away from Dwight. "And how is it any of your business whether or not I'm a Christian?"

"I am a representative of Jesus Christ," Dwight told him. "That makes your salvation my business."

The man stomped away shouting hateful and ugly words at Dwight. But three months later, at dawn on a cold, gray morning, Dwight heard a knock on his door.

"Who is there?" Dwight asked.

An unfamiliar voice answered. Dwight opened his door, and surprise flashed across his face when he saw the angry man from the lamppost standing before him.

"What brings you here?"

"I want to know how to become a Christian," the man begged. "Ever since that night, your words have haunted my every moment. I want to find Jesus so I can find peace."

Overwhelming joy flooded Dwight's heart as he prayed with the man. He loved seeing lives transformed, because he loved people. He wanted everyone to know the Savior who meant so much to him.

Dwight's passion to reach people sometimes led to unusual ministry techniques. To help attract children, he bought a little Indian pony. The pony walked the neighborhoods with Dwight, and they both became very popular. Dwight was often seen on "missionary journeys" with a child in his arms, a couple of children riding the pony, and a small army of children milling around him. His pockets were nearly always filled with fruit and sweet treats, and for a while he even walked around with a pet squirrel in a cage, which he later gave away to the child who brought the most visitors to Sunday School.

Although his methods were unconventional, Dwight had a special talent for reading people and seeing their potential. One summer, he promised thirteen young men new suits at Christmas if they would attend Sunday School faithfully that whole time. These were rough street boys, with names like "Red Eye" and "Madden the Butcher" and "Billy Bluecannon". No one believed they would be successful. No one, that is, except Dwight Moody.

When Christmas arrived, twelve of the thirteen boys had earned their suits! Dwight was proud of their success, and commended them publicly for their faithfulness. The boys loved Dwight for believing in them, and they became known as "Moody's Bodyguards", always defending their hero. When people called Dwight "Crazy Moody", as they often did, and when the newspapers made fun of him, "Moody's Bodyguards" were the first ones to come to his defense.

But then the war came, and Dwight's entire ministry changed.

A World at War

The Civil War came to Chicago when Camp Douglas was constructed just south of the city. Dwight had become intensely involved with the Chicago YMCA in addition to his Sunday School work, and he saw a perfect opportunity to integrate the work of the YMCA, the outreach of Sunday School, and the lives of soldiers. As soon as Camp Douglas was fully established, Dwight organized an Army and Navy Committee of the YMCA. Their goal was to reach out to soldiers with encouragement, support, and salvation.

The first mission of the new committee was to set up a temporary chapel for the soldiers at Camp Douglas, many of whom had grown up in Moody's Sunday Schools. In addition to conducting services and prayer meetings, Dwight and his fellow ministers gave out Bibles and hymn books for the soldiers and visited the men in their barracks, discouraging bad behavior. But the makeshift chapel was the centerpiece of the ministry, and over the course of the war more than 1,500 meetings were held there!

When the soldiers at Camp Douglas were all sent to the battlefield, they were replaced by 9,000 Confederate prisoners of war from the South. Although Dwight did not agree with some of the ideas the captured men held dear, he knew they needed Jesus. He decided to go and preach to the prisoners, and he asked his friend Edgar to come along.

As Dwight and Edgar neared the gates of Camp Douglas, Dwight realized how carefully the guards were checking everyone who went in and came out. Apparently the security had been increased when the prisoners had been moved there. Dwight knew Edgar did not have the proper documents to get into the camp, and many of the guards knew Dwight by sight. He decided he would have to hand off his generic ministerial pass to Edgar, who was also a minister, and hope that he could get in on recognition alone.

"Edgar," Dwight said softly as they drew near the gate, "I am going to give you my ministerial pass. It's the only way you will be allowed in."

Edger looked at Dwight in alarm. "How will you get in?"

"I believe I will find someone who knows me," he replied with a confidence he didn't feel. "But if I don't, you must go on without me."

Edgar tried to protest, but Dwight raised his hand and shook his head. His mind was made up. He handed Edgar the pass, and they approached the guards.

"Can I see your authorization to enter?"

Edgar held out the ministerial pass. The guard looked at it and nodded.

"Welcome to Camp Douglas," he said. Then he turned to Dwight. "Do you have a pass as well, sir?"

Dwight hesitated. "I have one, but it isn't with me at the moment. But I have spoken here many times before. My name is Dwight Lyman Moody."

The guard shook his head. "I'm sorry, sir. Without documentation, I cannot let you in. Those are the new rules."

"Of course…" Dwight said, his voice trailing off. Beside him, Edgar was beginning to sweat nervously. Dwight looked past the guard, hoping to see someone he knew. Suddenly, a familiar senior officer strolled into view.

"Captain!" Dwight called out. "Captain, over here!"

The captain turned and his face broke into a grin. He strode toward them and the guard snapped to attention.

"At ease, soldier," the captain said. "Dwight Moody! It's good to see you, my friend." They shook hands warmly. The captain turned to the guard. "Do you know who this is, young man?"

The guard shook his head.

"This is Mr. Moody," the captain informed him. "He is quite possibly the most famous preacher in Chicago and a good friend of this camp."

"He wants to enter without a pass, sir," the guard said. "Is that allowed?"

The captain hesitated. "Where is your pass?"

Dwight looked sideways at Edgar. The captain understood. He sighed.

"Because you have made such a difference in this camp, I will let you enter with a guard to escort you," the captain said. "But you must promise me you will be out of the camp by 8:00 p.m."

"I will do my best," Dwight promised.

"Don't just do your best," the captain cautioned. "If you are not out by 8:00, I will be forced to lock you up."

Edgar paled, but Dwight just grinned that old, charming grin. "Don't worry, Captain!"

It wasn't long before the familiar chapel was full and overflowing with Confederate prisoners. Dwight gave a stirring sermon, and when he saw tears on a number of faces, Dwight knew he had to give an invitation to salvation. As he began the invitation, Edgar leaned close to him.

"Dwight, it's already half past seven," he whispered. "If you do this, we'll never make it out in time."

"God is here!" Dwight whispered back. "How could I not invite them to meet Him?"

Dozens of men came forward for prayer and salvation, and Dwight and Edgar talked and prayed with each one. As they said goodbye to the last man, Edgar glanced at his pocket watch.

"It's 7:58, Dwight! We only have two minutes!"

Dwight snatched his Bible. "Run, Edgar," he cried. "Run like you've never run before!"

Edgar sprinted from the chapel toward the gate

with Dwight's portly figure not far behind. The guard couldn't help but giggle as the two men squeezed through the gate just as the clock struck eight. Then they collapsed, panting, both breathing sighs of relief.

This was the first of many meetings held for prisoners at the camp. Throughout the Civil War, Dwight preached to thousands and thousands of soldiers on both sides, and a great many souls came to Christ as a result.

One general wrote, "Crowds and crowds turned out to hear him. He showed them how a soldier could give his heart to God. His preaching was direct and effective, and multitudes responded with a promise to follow Christ."

Preaching at Camp Douglas was not the only evangelistic work Dwight did during the Civil War. He often traveled to battlefields and field hospitals to visit soldiers. The need for immediate salvation in the face of impending death gave an urgency to Dwight's messages that became a trademark of his ministry long after the war was over.

In April 1862, on a boat headed up the Tennessee River after the Battle of Pittsburgh Landing, Dwight was making his way through the decks, encouraging and witnessing to the wounded soldiers. In the corner of a deck, Dwight came alongside the bed of a badly injured soldier. He put a hand on the young man's shoulder.

"Can I pray over you, my boy?" he asked. Only silence answered him.

"He doesn't really talk," said the soldier in the next bed, propping himself up on his elbows to look at Dwight. "They say he won't last long. I heard the doctor and nurse talking this morning. They say he'll never make it back to Chicago."

"He's from Chicago?" Dwight asked. "I'm from Chicago! Perhaps he will hear if I pray for him, even if he cannot respond."

Dwight bowed his head, with his hand still on the soldier's shoulder, and offered a prayer. When he said, "Amen," the young man's eyes flickered halfway open.

"What is your name, boy?"

The young man's lips moved, but no sound came out. Finally, the soldier in the next bed spoke up again.

"His name is William Clark. He has a widowed mother and two little sisters back home."

Dwight leaned over the wounded soldier, whose eyes had fallen shut again.

"God bless you, William Clark," he murmured.

As Dwight turned to move on to another row of beds, a hand grasped his coat sleeve. He turned in surprise and saw William was struggling to sit, pulling Dwight toward him. Dwight bent over him.

"What is it, William?"

William swallowed hard, then whispered, "Can you—can you take a message to my mother for me?"

Dwight took William's weak hand in his own strong ones and said, "Of course. What shall I tell her?"

The peace of the Promised Land shone in William's smile. "Tell my mother that I died trusting in Jesus!"

By morning, William had gone to be with the Jesus he loved. And when they reached Chicago, Dwight's first objective was to find William's mother and give her his final message. With a little research, he found the house and sat with Mrs. Clark and her two young girls in a dim, tidy parlor. He told them how he had met William and how strong and brave William had been.

Then Dwight said, "Mrs. Clark, he had a special message for you. He had you in mind with the last words he spoke in this life. He asked me to assure you that he died trusting in Jesus. Mrs. Clark had been sitting straight and dry-eyed up to that point, but when Dwight gave the message from William, she looked at the floor. When she raised her head again, her cheeks were wet with tears, but her smile was radiant.

"Mr. Moody, in the midst of my great sorrow you have given me the greatest gift I could have ever received." She dabbed her eyes with a lacy handkerchief and added, "For as long as I can remember, William's salvation has been my most fervent prayer. And now you have given me hope and assurance that I will see my William again in Heaven someday. How can I ever thank you?"

As Dwight humbly explained that no thanks was required, there was a creak on the stairs. The two little girls, who had disappeared a few minutes earlier, shyly approached Dwight's chair.

"Mr. Moody," the oldest one said, "here is some money we have been saving for a very long time. We want to use it to honor William. Could you please use it to buy a Bible? I hope it is enough."

She held out a handful of coins, and her little sister did the same.

"Buy a Bible in William's honor, please, Mr. Moody," the little girl said. "Then give it to a soldier you meet so he can find Jesus just like William did."

Dwight cradled the coins as if they were pure gold. It was his turn to blink back emotion. Finally, he spoke.

"Mrs. Clark, it is I who should be thanking you. I came bearing a simple message, but you and your girls have ensured that I leave bearing a sacrifice of love."

Dwight was learning lessons around every bend in life's road, but there were even bigger lessons yet to come.

Daily Dedication

By the time the Civil War ended in 1865, Dwight Moody was in charge of the largest Sunday School in the United States, and people came from all corners of the country to study Dwight's methods. In 1860, before the Civil War even began, a Presidential candidate named Abraham Lincoln even came to tour the Sunday School in North Market Hall, and he commended Dwight on both his efforts and his success. Many others who came to visit and observe the Sunday School took what they learned back to their hometowns and started Sunday Schools of their own.

Dwight was becoming quite a celebrity, but he seemed oblivious to all the attention. He just kept doing what he had always done—working hard, seeking new Sunday School prospects, and reaching out to lost souls. He walked the neighborhoods with oranges, candy, maple sugar, and other treats, always looking for children to invite to Sunday School. He worked feverishly with the YMCA, organizing conventions, raising funds and speaking at meetings. He also hosted noon prayer meetings every day, drawing people from every realm of Chicago society.

In addition to all these tasks, Dwight took on a new responsibility right in the middle of the Civil War. On August 28th, 1862, Dwight married Emma Revell. He met Emma when she was a fifteen-year-old Sunday School teacher at the North Wells Street Sunday School, and they became friends. When Dwight decided to quit his sales job and go into full-time ministry work, Emma supported him wholeheartedly. He knew at that point that she was the one for him.

Dwight and Emma worked side-by-side in Sunday School work. It was tiring and thankless, but it was wonderful work. Dwight believed teachers should go beyond just teaching. He believed that teachers should make sure they were engaged in personal soul winning, making sure salvation was extended to every member of their class and beyond. At a Sunday School convention in the mid-1860s, he addressed a crowd of church workers on these convictions.

"If I had the trump of God, and could speak to every Sunday School teacher in America," Dwight said, "I would plead with each one to lead at least one soul to Christ this year!"

Dwight lived out what he believed in an open and obvious way. Even though the North Market Hall Sunday School had grown larger and incorporated into the Illinois Street Church, Dwight still operated just as he had when it was a fledgling Sunday School with dozens of pupils instead of hundreds. He saw every student as one of his personal charges. He visited them when they were absent and became deeply involved in their lives. In return, they were deeply devoted to him.

Dwight used this devotion to find opportunities to present the gospel. He also took baskets of food and clothing to poorhouses. As he distributed the items to those who were hungry and needy, Dwight shared Jesus with them. Many chose to accept Jesus as a direct result of Dwight's generosity and commitment, and the way his spirit reflected the heart of God.

On one of these visits Dwight met a mother with a young son. She was bedridden and close to death, but she called Dwight over to her bedside.

"My doctor tells me I won't be here much longer." Her voice quavered. "I know where I am going, but I am worried about my son. My husband is cruel and beats him, and I fear it will only grow worse when I am gone."

She looked up at Dwight, her eyes bright with anxious tears. "Mr. Moody, will you look after my son for me?"

Dwight promised he would, but when the mother passed away a few weeks later, the boy was nowhere to be found. Dwight sent several of his street-smart Sunday School boys out to search the city. Finally, one reported the boy was working as a bellhop at a local hotel.

Although it was late in the evening on July 3rd, the day before the Independence Day holiday, Dwight hurried down to the hotel. The boy was just finishing his shift.

"Is there somewhere we could talk privately?" Dwight asked after introducing himself.

The boy led Dwight to a corner of the rooftop. The faint scent of roofing tar hung in the warm summer night, and lights winked on and off in windows as Dwight and the boy stood side-by-side looking out over the city.

"Your mother asked me to watch over you when she was gone."

The boy stiffened. "I don't need anyone to watch over me. I can take care of myself."

"Don't you miss your mother's love and care?"

The boy bit his lip and looked away, quickly swiping away a wayward tear.

"Do you know there is One who loves you and cares for you even more than your mother ever did?"

The boy shook his head. So Dwight sat down on the rooftop and patted the ground beside him. When the boy sat, Dwight told him the story of Jesus and His love. He talked about the sacrifice of the cross. Tears ran freely down the boy's face in the darkness, as he realized he could still have the love he so desperately needed.

Finally, Dwight asked, "Would you like to give your life to Christ tonight? All you need to do is ask Him to forgive your sins and come into your life. Would you like to accept His gift of love and make Him the Lord of your life?"

The boy nodded, and they prayed together. As the prayer ended, Independence Day fireworks exploded around them like a celebratory fest of color and light and sound, heralding the miracle of salvation. Another lost soul had come home.

In addition to such evangelistic efforts, Dwight was widely known for his failure to be bound by what was "proper". When he was invited by prosperous businessmen to attend the opening of their new saloon, Dwight had a proposition for them.

"I will gladly come if I can bring a friend."

The men exchanged glances, and one said, "Mr. Moody, we would like you to be present, but this is not a religious occasion. No praying, please."

Dwight thought for a moment. "I promise not to pray at the opening if you will let me pray over you right now."

The men consented, and they all knelt with heads bowed. In his usual straightforward manner, Dwight prayed that God would bless the men. Then he prayed their saloon business would collapse, but they would all come to know Christ. The men looked up in alarm—it was not the prayer they had expected!

On another occasion, Dwight took the Sunday School children's choir to a local saloon. Dwight walked in with the group of children, and heads turned. Bleary eyes struggled to focus on Dwight.

"Would you fine gentlemen object to these young people singing a few songs for you?" he asked.

The men said no, and the choir sang a few patriotic songs. The men clapped and cheered heartily. Then the choir switched to a hymn and started passing out tracts.

"Now we will have a word of prayer," Dwight announced.

The saloon was instantly full of booing and jeers, but Dwight prayed anyway. When he finished, some of the men were sullen and angry, but others had tears on their faces.

"In a short while, we will have an evening service at North Market Hall," Dwight told the men. "We welcome you all to come."

To Dwight's surprise, nearly half of the men in the saloon left their seats and followed Dwight and his little choir to the service!

It was Dwight's habit to reach out to those who were often overlooked by "traditional" Christian workers. On summer evenings, he would set himself up in Chicago's Courthouse Square with a half dozen men and women as his choir. The choir would sing, and Dwight would preach. People passing by would stop to listen. Behind Dwight, the prisoners in the courthouse would crowd to their grated windows to listen, faces pressed against the bars to hear the service.

Opposition was frequent in these meetings. Critics would shout hateful things to disrupt the sermons. Drunkards would wander into the crowd and harass the people. One evening, a large clay pot was dropped from the upper floors of the courthouse, crashing down and shattering just a few feet from where Dwight stood. But Dwight was never afraid of opposition.

Never one to shy away from a challenge, Dwight recognized his roadblocks as signs that he was on the right track. And he believed this was just the beginning of what God wanted him to do. Big things were about to happen—Dwight was sure of it!

One Devoted Man

As part of his constant search for souls to change and lives to touch, Dwight was very active in the YMCA. In the 1800s, it was a strongly Christian organization, involved deeply in reaching lost young men and preparing them to live for the Savior. Dwight believed in this mission, and he ended up leading the Chicago YMCA as its president from 1865 to 1871.

Despite working with the YMCA, hosting noontime prayer meetings every day, and leading multiple church services every week, Dwight felt his ministry should be bigger and broader. He had heard of new ministry concepts being pioneered in England, and he greatly admired Charles Haddon Spurgeon and George Müller, both of whom worked in the United Kingdom. When Emma's doctor said a trip abroad might improve her severe asthma, Dwight seized the opportunity.

One bright Sunday morning in early 1867, Dwight announced to the church that he was leaving for England that week. Dwight and Emma packed their bags and headed from Chicago to New York. On

February 22nd, they set sail for England, beginning a whole new adventure in Dwight's ministry. They did not know what to expect, but they had faith that God was with them, and they knew He would lead them.

Dwight was not nearly as well known in England as he was in America, but the Secretary of the London Sunday School Union had heard Dwight speak during a visit to the United States. When he heard Dwight was in London, he invited him to speak at an anniversary meeting of the Sunday School Union. Dwight happily accepted the invitation.

Just before Dwight spoke, the chairman for the evening, a board member of the Sunday School Union, gave an introduction. "This is our American cousin," the man said, "the Reverend Mr. Moody of Chicago."

There was polite applause to this traditional and conventional introduction. But Dwight was never one for conventions. He leaped to his feet, climbed onto the platform, and immediately corrected the chairman.

"The chairman has made two mistakes," Dwight said. "To begin with, I'm not the 'Reverend' Mr. Moody at all. I'm plain Dwight L. Moody, a Sunday School worker. And then I'm not your 'American cousin'! By the grace of God, I'm your brother, who is interested with you in our Father's work for His children."

Dwight then launched into his message with fervor, and his listeners sat spellbound. They were shocked into silence by his blatant honesty and disregard for conventions.

Within a few weeks of his arrival, Dwight found his way to the London YMCA. He asked if he could establish a noon prayer meeting there, just as he had in Chicago. They agreed. On May 13th, 1867, the first noontime prayer meeting was held at the London YMCA with nearly a hundred men in attendance. Soon the daily attendance was between 200 and 300, and other noontime meetings were popping up all over the United Kingdom. Unconventional as he was, Dwight was starting a cultural movement!

During the few months he remained in the United Kingdom on this trip, Dwight traveled widely, hoping to discover a broad representation of the Christian methods at work there. In one city, he heard the words that would come to shape his ministry for the rest of his life.

"The world has yet to see," a pastor said, "what God can do with and for and through and in and by the man who is fully and wholly consecrated to Him."

Dwight deeply pondered those words that night.

"He said a man," Dwight reasoned. "He did not say a great man or an educated man or a rich man or a wise man or an eloquent man or a smart man. I am a man, and I decide for myself how consecrated I will be. From this day forward, I will try my utmost to be that one devoted man God is seeking, serving Him with all that I have and all that I am."

Near the end of his trip, while on a visit to Dublin, Ireland, Dwight met another devoted man, a young prizefighter-turned-preacher named Henry Moorehouse. Henry was eager to preach in new places and to new people, and he begged Dwight to let him travel back to America with the Moody family. He wanted to preach in Dwight's church in Chicago, but Dwight thought he was just an overeager boy. To be kind, he told Henry to contact him if he ever made it to America. Dwight assumed that was the last he would hear of Henry Moorehouse.

In early July, just before returning to America with his family, Dwight spoke at the annual breakfast of the London YMCA. Later, at a reception held for the Moody family, one of the speakers gave a tribute to Dwight.

"He came to England unknown and unloved," the speaker began. "But after just a few short months, he is leaving us widely known and dearly loved. He is a committed man, and people can't help but catch his vision."

Dwight traveled home to Chicago with many fond memories of his trip. Little did he know, one of his memories from the United Kingdom was about to follow him to Chicago.

Moorehouse's Messages

The Moody family was warmly welcomed back to Chicago, and Dwight settled back into his busy routines. But only a few weeks had passed before he received an unexpected letter from Henry Moorehouse. Henry said he was in America and would like to come and see Dwight in Chicago.

Dwight sighed. He thought he had adequately discouraged Henry in Dublin, but apparently he had been wrong. Dwight wrote a quick, impersonal note to Henry, saying, "If you come west, call on me." A few more weeks passed, and Dwight received another letter from Henry.

"I am still in America," Henry wrote, "and I would be happy to come to preach in Chicago if you want me."

Again, Dwight sent a brief, impersonal note, saying, "If you happen to come west, drop in on me."

Within a few days, communication came from Henry that he would be in Chicago the following Thursday. Dwight was surprised. He had not expected Henry to be so persistent or to make the more than

1,000-mile trip to Chicago. Dwight was scheduled to be in meetings out of town that Thursday and Friday, and he wasn't convinced Henry could preach. He decided to take the matter to his church officers.

"He is a nice young man," Dwight told the officers. "He seems very devoted to the work of God. I'm just not sure of his abilities."

"Have you ever heard him preach?" one officer asked.

"No," Dwight admitted.

"I think it is too great a risk," another officer said.

"But he could be a great preacher," countered the first officer. "We will never know unless we give him a try."

Dwight thought for a few minutes. "Everyone has to start somewhere. Let him speak on Thursday. It is an 'off' night, and crowds will likely be small. If he does poorly, he will have had his chance. If he does well, announce him as the speaker for the regular Friday night prayer meeting."

"And if he does well on Friday night?"

Dwight shrugged. "Announce him as the speaker for Sunday, I suppose."

Dwight left for his out-of-town meetings on Thursday morning, putting his full faith in the church officers. When he returned on Saturday, the first thing he asked Emma was how she liked Henry's preaching.

"The people loved his preaching, and I enjoyed it too," she told him. "He preached two sermons, both from the text of John 3:16."

"Two sermons on John 3:16? I wouldn't have thought that was possible," Dwight remarked, unpacking some of his things from the well-worn travel bag.

"Well, he preaches a little…differently than you do."

Dwight raised his head to look at Emma. "What do you mean 'differently'?"

Emma hesitated. "For one thing, he preaches that God loves the worst sinners."

"Well then, he's wrong," Dwight snapped. "God extends judgment to sinners, not love."

"You just might change your mind," Emma cautioned, stifling a smile. "He supports everything he says with scriptures."

As people began to arrive for the service the next morning, Dwight noticed they all had Bibles with them, which was unusual. Dwight usually preached from a single text, so carrying a Bible was largely unnecessary. As he listened to Henry preach, he understood why they had their Bibles. Once again, Henry preached from John 3:16, but support for his main ideas came from various parts of scripture, and the people were eagerly searching out each verse.

In the evening service, Henry again preached from John 3:16, this time focusing on God's expression of love for mankind throughout history—first through the patriarchs, then the prophets, then Jesus Christ and the Holy Spirit. Dwight was transfixed in his seat, and he felt tears pricking his eyelids. It was the first time he had fully realized the true depths of God's love. He felt like his heart was melting within him.

When Henry preached from John 3:16 yet again on Monday night, Dwight's transformation was complete. He shared his thoughts with Emma after the service that evening.

"For so long, I have preached the wrath of God against sinners, instead of His great love for them," Dwight admitted. "But now I see that love is a greater power than anger. There is one thing that draws above everything else in this world, and that is love."

The crowds packed the hall every night to hear Henry speak, and every night he took them to John 3:16 as their text. On the seventh night, Henry took the platform with a grin.

"Beloved friends," he began, "I have been hunting all day for a new text." He paused for effect. "But I could not find anything so good as the old one. So, please turn in your Bibles to John 3:16."

The congregation chuckled good-naturedly and turned to the familiar passage.

When the campaign was over, Henry and Dwight exchanged a warm handshake. They had developed quite a friendship, and Henry promised to come again soon. True to his word, Henry returned the following year, and he and Dwight conducted more than seventy meetings in several different cities.

When Henry was gone, Dwight returned to his old duties with new vigor and purpose, eager to communicate God's love with the world around him. One of his primary mission fields was the noontime prayer meeting each day at the Chicago YMCA. People from all walks of life attended these meetings, from the poorest day laborers to the richest business owners.

In addition to the prayer meetings, Dwight also spoke at special meetings, attended conventions, and organized services. He was very busy, but he loved the sheer number of people he was able to meet and minister to, sharing Jesus in every aspect of life. And he never hesitated to use his old skills as a salesman to raise funds for the YMCA.

Thanks in large part to Dwight's fundraising efforts—and a generous partnership with businessman John W. Farwell—the first YMCA meeting hall in the United States was erected in Chicago in 1867. Dubbed Farwell Hall, the auditorium could seat 3,000 people. For the dedication service on September 29th, 1867, there was standing room only. Dwight gave an energizing sermon, encouraging everyone in attendance to do great things for God.

Sadly, only four months after the dedication service, Farwell Hall burned to the ground. Dwight faced this obstacle head on, just as he did with every difficulty. He loved a challenge, and within four more months, funds had been raised and a whole new Farwell Hall had been built on the rubble of the old one! Even on the darkest days, Dwight never lost sight of the promise of Luke 1:47, "For with God nothing shall be impossible."

Moody and Sankey

At the conventions he attended, Dwight loved to share his stories of God doing the impossible. At the YMCA convention in Indianapolis in 1870, Dwight was a popular speaker, sharing endless stories of the work he had seen God do. He was scheduled to lead an early morning meeting near the end of the convention, and when the time came for the meeting to start, the large meeting hall was crowded with people hoping to hear Dwight speak. As the minutes ticked by and the start time came and went, the song leader had still not arrived.

A stickler for starting on time, Dwight was becoming agitated. He knew he was not much of a singer and could certainly not lead a large group in song. Exasperated, he stepped to the front of the platform, and all eyes turned toward him.

"Is there anyone here who feels able to lead the group in song?"

All around the hall, men looked at one another uncomfortably. They were preachers and teachers and administrators, not singers. Then, near the back of the room, a tall, kind-faced man with bushy eyebrows and a broad mustache stood to his feet.

"There is a fountain filled with blood," he began in a rich, robust baritone, "drawn from Emmanuel's veins…"

Within moments, the hall was alive with song as everyone joined in the well-loved hymn. The walls reverberated with the sound of voices lifted in praise. Dwight smiled with satisfaction, and the service went on, powerful and profound.

After the service, Dwight greeted the participants at the door. Toward the end of the line, the tall man came by and shook Dwight's hand. Dwight recognized him immediately.

"You are my impromptu song leader," Dwight said warmly. "I am so thankful for your assistance today. What is your name, sir?"

"I am Ira Sankey," the man replied. "And I am the one who was blessed today. I am always thankful for the opportunity to use my voice for my Lord."

"Tell me, Mr. Sankey," Dwight prodded, "where are you from? What do you do for a living? Do you have a family?"

Ira Sankey was a bit overwhelmed by this flood of questions. "I am a businessman from back east," he said. "I am a single man, so I mostly spend my time in business and in my work with the YMCA."

Dwight smiled. "Well, you'll have to give all that up! You are the man I have been looking for, and I want you to come to Chicago and help me in my work."

"I can't just walk away from my whole life," Ira protested. "I believe in what you are doing, Mr. Moody. I believe in it with my whole heart. But I'm not sure it's what God has called me to do. What you are asking me to do—well, it is just so..."

Dwight realized he had perhaps come on a bit too forcefully. He knew deep in his soul that Ira Sankey was the ministry partner he had prayed for. Now he had to wait patiently for God to reveal that to Ira. Dwight quickly changed his approach.

"Would you be willing to meet me for lunch today to discuss the matter further?"

Ira agreed, and over lunch, Dwight told him more about the ministries in Chicago and what the needs were. Ira was still unconvinced, but he promised to pray about the opportunity.

"That's all I ask," said Dwight with a grin. "I have faith that God will do the convincing."

Later that day, Dwight sent a note to Ira by messenger. The note asked Ira to meet him on a designated street corner that afternoon to help with an open-air meeting. Ira wrote back, "I'll be there!"

When Ira reached the street corner just before the arranged time, he found Dwight perched on a wooden crate. Dwight's face brightened when he saw Ira.

"I'm so glad you could come, friend," Dwight said. "Let's get started. Could you lead out with a few hymns?"

Ira began a song, and his velvety voice carried from corner to corner, drawing people in. Hymn rolled into hymn, and by the time the singing was over, a sizeable crowd had gathered. As Dwight began speaking, the crowd continued to grow. Men were coming home from the mills and factories, and Dwight's passionate preaching pulled them from the streets and brought many to tears.

After speaking for only about twenty minutes, Dwight ended with a short prayer. Then he invited the crowd to join him for another meeting at the Academy of Music just down the road.

"Start us on 'Shall We Gather,' please, Mr. Sankey," Dwight instructed.

Ira's baritone came alive with, "Shall we gather at the river, where bright angel feet have trod…"

The crowd joined in, and with voices lifted high, they marched through the streets to the Academy of Music, a thundering, formidable army of joy and salvation. Ira felt God's Spirit surrounding him, and he began to wonder if working with Dwight might be a part of God's plan for him after all.

A few months later, Ira agreed to visit Chicago to see Dwight's ministries firsthand. He arrived at the Moody residence as Dwight, Emma, and their small children were having morning devotions. Dwight welcomed him warmly and made introductions all around.

"Have a seat at the organ, Ira," Dwight insisted. "Lead us in a hymn before we start our day."

When the singing was done, Dwight and Ira headed out into the city. They spent the day visiting sick church members. At each stop, Dwight would pray and Ira would sing. It was amazing to see faces tight with pain relaxing in peace as prayer and song soothed the soul. By the end of the day, Ira was both exhausted and inspired.

The pace never slowed. Dwight was tireless, and every day brought a new ministry challenge and a new way to share Jesus with the people of Chicago. Ira's visit culminated in a huge service on Sunday at Farwell Hall. He led the singing and Dwight preached. As Ira sang the invitation hymn, he watched the aisles crowd with people coming to give their lives to Jesus. In that moment, he fully understood what motivated Dwight to work so fervently.

When Ira's visit was over, he bid the Moody family an emotional goodbye. After only a week, he felt like a member of the family.

"Remember the need you have seen this week, my friend," Dwight urged as they parted. "I cannot do this work alone. I hope you will make up your mind to come as soon as possible."

Ira laughed at Dwight's persistence, but he knew Dwight was right about the need. Within a few weeks, Ira resigned his business and moved to Chicago. The team of Dwight and Ira soon became known as "Moody and Sankey," and their popularity spread like wildfire. Invitations came in for speaking engagements all around the country, and Dwight jumped at the chance of a broader adventure.

The Great Chicago Fire

In the early summer of 1871, Moody and Sankey returned from a lengthy speaking trip in California. Chicago was deep in the smothering clutches of a heat wave, and church attendance had dropped off significantly. Dwight knew he had to bring his people back to church before they lost all desire to get together.

He tried to think of some gimmick to bring people in. Should he arrange a concert? Would people attend a historical lecture? After much thought and prayer, Dwight decided to preach a series on Bible characters. He began with Adam and worked his way through Enoch, Noah, Abraham, and so on.

The series was a hit, and Farwell Hall began to fill again. When he reached the life of Christ, Dwight decided to take six weeks to tell the story. He wanted to make sure his listeners fully understood who Jesus was. He wanted to ignite a passion in them to share Jesus with those around them.

On the fifth Sunday of the series about Christ, Dwight's topic was, "What Then Shall I Do with

Jesus Which Is Called the Christ?" It was an evening service, and Farwell Hall was packed with the largest crowd Dwight had ever preached to in Chicago. He preached with all his heart, urging the crowd to decide for themselves what they would do with Jesus in their own lives.

As the service came to a close, Dwight said, "Each one must make a decision for Jesus individually. I will not ask you to make such a serious decision tonight. Go home. Think it over this week. Then come back next week and be saved."

Dwight nodded to Ira, and he began the closing song, "Today the Savior Calls". But as the song ended, a new and plaintive melody of sirens and warning bells was rising from the streets and bouncing off the buildings. The air outside was bitter with smoke that hung in an ominous cloud over Chicago, and an eerie glow came from deep within the city. The crowd dispersed quickly, and Dwight hurried home. The Great Chicago Fire had begun.

For a while, deep in the night, it looked like the Fire Department had the upper hand. The warning bells stopped ringing, and Dwight and Emma breathed a sigh of relief and went to bed. But only an hour later, the warning bells rang again and the cry went out to evacuate. The fire had jumped the river and was devouring buildings faster than the Fire Department could fight back. It was headed straight for the Moodys' neighborhood.

Dwight grabbed his two small children and ran outside. A neighbor was just loading his carriage, and he offered to take the children to safety. Dwight kissed their sleepy faces and handed them over. Then he ran back into the house and called for Emma. He threw a few sentimental gifts from friends and a few household valuables into a baby carriage.

"Emma, dear," Dwight called, an urgent note creeping into his voice, "we have to go. Are you ready?"

"Just one more thing. We have to take your portrait."

Dwight came into the hall and found Emma trying to wrestle a huge oil portrait of Dwight off the wall. He knew it was her most prized possession, but he also recognized how hard it would be to carry as they fled.

"Emma, you have to leave it. We have to go."

"I won't leave it," she muttered, her small frame twisting in determination. "Just help me get it down."

Dwight put a compassionate hand on her shoulder. "And then what? We can't carry that with us."

"You could carry it," she said defiantly.

Dwight began to giggle. Then he laughed out loud. Emma stopped her work to glare at him.

"What's so funny?"

"Just imagine that we meet a friend or neighbor in the street as we escape," Dwight said, chuckling. "He will ask what dear possession I felt I could not live without. And I will be forced to reveal that my most valuable possession is a picture of myself!" Dwight laughed out loud again. "Imagine what kind of man I will look like!"

Emma's lips twitched in an involuntary smile. She ran off to the kitchen and grabbed a knife from a drawer. In an instant, she had carefully cut the canvas away from the frame. She quickly rolled it up and threw it over her shoulder. It was almost as big as she was!

"I can't carry it in the frame, but I can carry it this way," she insisted. "And if you won't save it, I will!"

She hefted the awkward roll a bit higher on her shoulder and headed for the door. A very amused Dwight followed her, grinning and shaking his head.

The Moodys lost their home that night. The Illinois Street Church and Farwell Hall both burned to the ground. In fact, the Great Chicago Fire burned for nearly two whole days—from October 8th to 10th, 1871—leaving death and destruction in its wake. When it was all over, more than 300 people had died, and more than 100,000 were left homeless.

On the morning after the fire ended, Dwight stood at a second story window in a friend's house, looking out over his smoldering city. Emma brought him a cup of tea and stood beside him. She knew well the look in Dwight's eyes.

"What are you thinking?" she asked.

"That I need to help…somehow."

The sunlight played on Emma's dark hair as she sipped her tea. "Where will you go?"

"Back East. There will be people there— businessmen—with funds to help." He turned to face her. "Will you and the children be alright here for a while?"

Emma squeezed his hand. "We'll be fine. Do whatever God is telling you to do."

Dwight traveled throughout the East, visiting large cities and small towns. He preached and begged and pleaded. Within two months, he had raised enough to build a 75-by-100-foot temporary building. It was quickly constructed and dedicated as the Northside Tabernacle on Christmas Eve, 1871.

Dwight also raised money to help families who were homeless and other churches and groups that needed to rebuild. But as he traveled, he realized he needed to take a break from teaching and preaching and spend some time learning from others. And he knew just where to do it.

Abroad Again

Although the spiritual climate of England was cold during the 1870s, there were several great Bible teachers there, and Dwight felt he had much to learn from them. In June 1872, Dwight traveled to England again. But his goal this time was not to preach and teach, but to be preached and taught to, learning all he could. He also wanted to do some evangelistic work. There were people who remembered Dwight and his unconventional style from his visit five years earlier, however, and speaking engagements had to occasionally be arranged.

One Sunday, Dwight was asked to preach in North London. The morning service was cold and dull, stifled by formality and tradition. But the evening service seemed filled with the Holy Spirit. Dwight shared his heart and spoke the story of Jesus with such passion that the whole congregation was moved. At the end of the service, Dwight asked anyone interested in salvation to stand. Nearly the entire congregation rose!

Thinking they must be confused, Dwight asked those who were truly interested in salvation to follow him to a smaller room for prayer. The people packed the little room and spilled out through the door. Dwight spoke and prayed with as many as he could. He told the rest to come back the next night to speak with the pastor. They agreed.

On Monday morning, Dwight left for Dublin, Ireland for another scheduled engagement. But on Tuesday, he received word from the pastor in North London that even more people had come on Monday night. The pastor was overwhelmed, and he was begging for Dwight's help. Excitement mounted in Dwight's heart as he hurried back to London. Dwight held ten days of meetings at the North London church, and more than 400 people were saved!

Later, Dwight learned of a contributing factor—he believed—to the success of those meetings. Within the North London church, there were two sisters. One was bedridden due to a serious illness, but she was active in prayer for her church. Nearly a year before Dwight came to North London, this girl had read about his meetings in America. She began right then to pray every day that God would bring Dwight Moody to her church, and she shared her prayers with her sister.

On that first Sunday morning when Dwight preached, the sister came home and said, "You'll never guess who spoke in the service this morning…"

"Who?" the sister asked eagerly, leaning forward in her bed.

"Dwight L. Moody!"

A wave of joy rolled across the girl's face as she leaned back with a smile. "Do you know what this means? It means God has heard my prayers! A great revival is coming!"

When Dwight heard of the girl's faithfulness in prayer, his heart was deeply touched. He was again reminded that every person has a part to play in accomplishing the work of God. A few weeks later, Dwight returned to the United States with his passion refreshed and his heart ready to work.

The trip home to America was fairly short-lived, and within a few months, Dwight, Emma, their children, and Ira Sankey were all headed back to the United Kingdom at the invitation of three prominent pastors. The pastors had promised to pay the expenses for the trip, but when the departure date arrived, funds had still not been sent. Dwight used some of his savings to purchase tickets, and Ira and the Moody family set out for Liverpool, England.

When they arrived, Dwight learned why the funds had not come. All three pastors who had invited Dwight had died before the trip. Unsure of God's direction in the face of such unexpected news, the travelers rented a room for the night. It seemed the British door had closed suddenly, and Dwight felt a little lost.

"God, please show me Your plan," he silently prayed. "I desperately need Your direction tonight."

As he took off his coat to prepare for bed that evening, Dwight saw something flutter to the ground. He stooped to pick it up and realized it was an unopened letter. He remembered that it had come to him just before they sailed from New York, and in the haste of departure, he had stuffed it—unread—into his pocket. With mounting excitement, Dwight tore open the letter. It was an invitation from Mr. Bennett, the YMCA Secretary at York, asking Dwight to come speak there if he ever found himself in England again.

"This door is only ajar," Dwight told Emma and Ira after reading them the letter, "but we will consider this letter as God's hand leading to York, and we will go there."

"Dwight," Emma said when they were alone, "perhaps the children and I should stay in London with my sister."

"I think that would be wise," Dwight agreed. "There may be a great deal of traveling from place to place, and it could be hard on the little ones."

The next morning, Emma and the children left for her sister's house, and Dwight and Ira headed to York. Mr. Bennett had warned them the city was spiritually cold and dead, and that was exactly how they found it. Four churches agreed to let Dwight preach from their pulpits.

"I am ready to go in at once," Dwight told Mr. Bennett. "It is true the city seems cold and dead, but we serve a God who specializes in transforming hearts that are cold and dead."

Handbills and flyers were quickly prepared and distributed throughout York. The first service was held the next day, on Sunday, June 22nd, 1873, at the Salem Congregational Chapel. It was a modest crowd of Christian workers from around the city. Later that day, Dwight preached in the large hall at the Corn Exchange, and nearly 1,000 people showed up! To finish the day, Dwight spoke at an evening service at the Wesley Chapel.

Bible lectures were offered every night that week, and their popularity grew with each service. By the following Sunday, Dwight preached four separate services, with over 3,000 attending that day. News began to spread throughout the region that God was doing a great work in York through Moody and Sankey's preaching and singing. Invitations arrived from all around the United Kingdom, begging the team to come and minister in all types of churches.

As more and more people were exposed to his sermons, Dwight's knowledge of and frequent references to Bible passages caused a run on Bibles. The demand was so great the British Bible publishers struggled to keep pace. The dramatic impact of God's Word puzzled Dwight's critics, but it fueled his fire, deepening his desire to do bigger and better things for God. He couldn't wait to see what God would do next!

English Adventures

After five weeks in York, Dwight accepted an invitation to Sunderland. His reputation preceded him, and after just a few meetings, the crowd overflowed the chapel. The attendance continued to grow every service, until finally Dwight was forced to move to Victoria Hall, one of the largest halls in Northern England.

"These crowds surprise me," commented Mr. Rees, the pastor who had invited Moody and Sankey to Sunderland. "I must admit, I did not expect the two of you to have such a pull."

"Why not?"

"Well," Mr. Rees said, "I had heard that Mr. Moody talked too fast and told too many personal stories. I had also heard he was uneducated, and not the least bit poetic or eloquent."

Dwight grinned. It wasn't anything he hadn't heard before. "And what do you think now?"

"You do talk too fast and tell a lot of stories," Mr. Rees said. "But you seldom utter a sentence that is not well worth hearing. You are earnest, courageous, and untiring, and your love for souls is obvious. I find you both to be genuine to the backbone."

It was an opinion shared by many. Dwight and Ira were causing quite a stir in the religious community. People who had not attended church in years were coming to see these two Americans with their simple, straightforward style.

From Sunderland, Moody and Sankey moved on to Newcastle-upon-Tyne. While they were there, a Member of Parliament named Cohen wrote an article describing their meetings as "a wonderful religious phenomenon". This brought new attention from the elite and educated classes, compounding their popularity. The meetings at Newcastle soon outgrew the 1,600-seat auditorium at the Rye Hill Baptist Church, and the remaining meetings were moved to a music hall, the largest building in town.

At one of these meetings, Dwight met a lady who wanted to be saved, but wasn't sure she could be.

"Why do you think you can't be saved?" Dwight asked.

"Years ago, I was a housekeeper for a very rich man. I stole five bottles of wine from him. I don't think he ever knew, but every time I close my eyes to pray, all I can see are those five wine bottles. What should I do?"

Dwight thought for a moment, silently praying for the best answer. "You must pay him for the wine."

"I can't," the lady said, her voice heavy with remorse. "He has been dead for years."

"Does he have any living heirs?"

She nodded. "He has a son still living."

"Then go to his son and pay for the wine," Dwight advised.

"I cannot do that, sir," she said. "I am an upstanding lady in my community now. How can I admit before my friends and neighbors that I am a thief?"

She turned and walked away with her shoulders slumped hopelessly. Dwight watched her go with a twinge of sadness. The next night, she was back.

"I thought about what you said," she told Dwight.

"So, are you going to talk with the man's son?"

"No, I still can't do that." She paused and eyed Dwight hopefully. "But I was wondering if I could just put the amount I owe in the collection plate and give it to God."

"God doesn't want stolen money," Dwight answered bluntly. "You must go make this right if you ever want to have peace."

She left angry and resistant. Dwight looked for her the next night, but she did not attend the meeting that night or the next. It was several days before Dwight glimpsed her again, making her way across the room. She pushed eagerly through the crowd to where he stood.

"Mr. Moody, it worked!" she exclaimed. A joyous smile lit her face and the lines of tension and guilt had smoothed. "I went to the son of my old employer and told him everything. At first he tried to refuse the money I offered, but I insisted he must take it, and he finally did. And once I had his forgiveness, I prayed and asked God to forgive me—not just for that sin, but for all my sins!'"

"And how do you feel now?"

She sighed happily. "I am finally at peace with God and with myself."

Similar scenes were repeated often during these campaigns. God used Dwight's words and Ira's songs to encourage, inspire, and convict the hearers. And souls that had long been stagnant came alive with new passion and power.

The coordination of Ira's songs with the themes of Dwight's messages was instrumental in reaching souls. But the American songs Ira sang—along with a number of original songs he had written—were not in the British hymnals. As the songs became more popular, the need for a new hymnal became obvious. A sixteen-page booklet called "Sacred Songs and Solos" was created, followed a few months later by a small book with just the words of the songs for congregational use.

This little hymnal was used in many of the services, and the participation of the people greatly enriched the experience. Momentum was building, and Dwight and Ira could feel the Spirit of God with them, empowering their work. It was a necessary power, because their leisurely trip through England was about to explode into something much bigger than they had ever expected!

Saving Scotland

After seeing the results in the English cities and towns, several pastors in Edinburgh, Scotland invited Moody and Sankey to come and minister there. The first service was held in the largest music hall in the city on November 23rd, 1873. Dwight had been ill the night before, and Ira's organ was broken, but they trusted God to bless the service.

By the time the service started, every seat was full, and people were crammed into every square foot of standing room. They squeezed into lobbies, doorways, and stairwells. Outside, several thousand were turned away for lack of room. And the numbers only increased from there!

Every evening that week, more than 2,000 people crowded into the Barclay Free Church. The next Sunday, three services were held in three different churches. Each one was full long before service time, and several hundred were turned away from each location. By the third week, the numbers were even greater. The people were flocking to hear the simple message of God's love and what it could mean to them.

In addition to the nightly meetings and multiple services on Sundays, Dwight established noontime prayer meetings in Edinburgh, as he did in every city he visited. Every day at noon, more than 500 believers met to pray over the hundreds of requests that came in. They met for an hour, had singing and Bible reading, heard prayer requests, prayed together, and shared testimonies of God's goodness in their lives. After only a few weeks of these meetings, the attendance had grown to over a thousand each day!

Through the dedicated team of Moody and Sankey, God was reaching the multitudes. Converts ranged from pudgy, round-faced children to stooped, wrinkled old men; from disciplined castle soldiers to rebellious university students. The same love and grace were extended to the rich and the poor, the educated and the uneducated, the skeptics, the drunkards, the backsliders, and the outcasts. All could come to Jesus and find salvation—and many of them did.

God was clearly doing big things in Edinburgh. But with spiritual victories come spiritual battles, new and brutal. A Scottish businessman from Chicago sent a letter to a number of prominent church leaders in Edinburgh and throughout Scotland. The letter accused Dwight of dishonest and fraudulent business practices, false religious claims, and other vices and crimes.

One of the church leaders in Edinburgh brought a copy of the letter to Dwight.

"I thought you should see this," he said. "All of the church leaders in Scotland have received it, and it has been widely circulated in public forums."

Dwight took the letter, and as he read it, his face paled. Then his jaw set in characteristic determination.

"These things are not true," he insisted.

"Of course they aren't. We all realize that. No one believes this. We know what kind of man you are."

Dwight drew a deep breath. "Believing in my integrity is not enough. You must investigate these charges and accusations and prove them false. Otherwise, Satan will continue to use this against me."

He turned to the church leader, his eyes wide and pleading. "Will you please get together a group of church leaders here in Edinburgh to thoroughly investigate these accusations?"

Seeing his earnestness, the church leader lay a hand on Dwight's shoulder. "I'll see to it right away."

The Edinburgh Committee, as the investigative group called themselves, immediately wrote to Dwight's friend and upstanding Chicago businessman, John W. Farwell. They sent a copy of the slanderous letter and asked for Farwell's thoughts and opinions.

A reply soon came from Chicago. John Farwell said upon hearing the attack on Dwight's character and reading the letter, he had conducted a thorough investigation throughout Chicago. Farwell had a broad scope of influence, and he could find no one with a negative impression of Dwight. The reply sent to Edinburgh was signed by thirty-five pastors, educators, editors, and secretaries. They said Dwight was "evangelical and Christian in the highest sense of those terms."

"We do not hesitate," the reply went on, "to commend him as an earnest Christian worker, worthy of the confidence of our Scotch and English brethren, with whom he is now laboring, believing that the Master will be honored by them in receiving him among them as a co-laborer in the vineyard of the Lord."

With that glowing response, both Dwight and his critics were satisfied, and the ministry moved rapidly forward.

One of the greatest services in Edinburgh was the Watch-night Service at the Free Assembly Hall, the largest building in Edinburgh, on December 31st, 1873. The service was scheduled to begin at 8:00 p.m., but by 7:00 p.m., the hall was packed. The crowd buzzed with anticipation until finally—promptly at 8:00—Dwight and a team of pastors entered the hall.

After several songs were sung and an opening prayer was offered, Dwight announced the evening would be fully participatory. Anyone in the congregation could present anything that qualified as worship. The night was full of variety, with singing, testifying, reciting, and reading. Many of the people present participated, and it was a full and exciting service.

At 11:00 p.m., Dwight called for quiet. "Thank you all for your participation," he said. "It has truly blessed my heart and the hearts of all present. Now, let us come together to pray. We will give thanks for the old year and pray for God's blessings and guidance over the New Year."

As the New Year began, the services in Edinburgh continued to grow. One night, Donald McAllan, a man who hated everything related to God, came to a service at the Free Assembly Hall to argue with Dwight. After the service, Donald approached Dwight and made a remark about the worthlessness of salvation and how God plays favorites, hoping to make Dwight angry.

Dwight turned to him with fire in his eyes, but love in his voice. "Have you ever known someone that tried to come to Christ and was refused?"

"No," said Donald. "But what good is the promise or the favor of a God we cannot see or hear or touch?"

"I serve a God who is faithful," Dwight said. "And He hasn't broken a promise to me yet!"

Donald had no reply, and Dwight studied him carefully with a twinkle in his eye. "Do you know we are praying for you, friend?" he said. "And you will yet be converted!"

A few weeks later, Donald came to another meeting and argued with Dwight. But at the third meeting he attended, God touched Donald's heart, and he gave his life to Christ. As the story of Donald McAllan's conversion spread throughout the city, many people doubted it, and some even called it lies and propaganda. People in Edinburgh knew Donald McAllan—he was outspoken about his beliefs—and they didn't believe he could ever become a Christian.

Dwight heard these rumors and remarks and wanted to prove the power of God. So one night, at a service at the Free Assembly Hall—the very place where Donald McAllan had experienced his transformation—Dwight told the whole story to his captive audience.

He ended the story by saying, "I understand that this former infidel is present in this meeting. If so, will he kindly rise and bear witness to the fact of his conversion?"

There was an extended moment of prolonged silence as the people looked around. Finally, Donald McAllan stood, and every head swiveled his way.

"It's true. I am a Christian now," he confirmed. Then he shared the story of how God had touched his heart and what God had done for him.

The ministry at Edinburgh kept growing, but Dwight knew it was time to move on. Plans were already in place for ministry in Glasgow, Scotland. But even Dwight could not imagine the big ways God would work there!

God's Work in Glasgow

The first service in Glasgow was on February 8th, 1874. At 9:00 a.m., 3,000 Sunday School teachers and workers gathered to hear Dwight speak. It was a big kickoff for what would prove to be a big campaign. The evening service was much larger than the morning service, and soon Glasgow City Hall was not large enough to hold the crowds.

Because of the number of people involved, Glasgow became a center of outreach to the smaller towns and cities throughout the region. Thousands of people were reached for Christ through Dwight's extended ministry. Dwight was determined that God's message would not be hindered by a lack of space or transportation. He pledged that if the people couldn't get to the gospel, he would take the gospel to them.

In addition to the outreach ministries, Dwight led large meetings in Glasgow. He also held a month-long convention of pastors, church leaders, and believers. The purpose was to fuel revival and find ways to preserve that spirit of revival throughout Scotland. To make sure there was enough space, the convention was held at the Botanical Gardens, which had a hall that could hold thousands.

The first service had more than 5,000 Christian workers in attendance. There were also meetings for young men, young women, and children, all of which had more than 6,000 in attendance. Dwight tried to hold meetings for every group and class of people because the gospel is for everyone. He believed it was his job to reach out to everyone, just as Jesus did.

The grand finale of the convention was a massive, all-inclusive service on a Sunday afternoon. Between 20,000 and 30,000 people showed up to hear Dwight speak! No one had expected crowds that large. When Ira Sankey arrived, he made his way into the large building and began the worship service.

There were 7,000 people packed into the hall, and their voices were thunderous when lifted in praise. Ira led them in hymn after hymn. When they had sung several songs, Ira began to look around anxiously. Where was Dwight? It was unlike him to be late for a service. Ira wondered if something was wrong.

Outside the building, Dwight was getting frustrated. He had pulled up in his carriage a few minutes late, and he was unable to get through the crowds into the hall. Every entrance was packed solid, and people were wedged into every space, elbow to elbow, so they could barely move, even if they wanted to. Dwight did not even have a good way to get word to Ira of his plight. Finally, Dwight decided to make the best of a bad situation.

"Driver, could you pull over here, please?" Dwight asked.

When the carriage was in the center of the broad drive, Dwight climbed up on the coachman's box.

"This will do," he said, his eyes scanning the crowd. "You there—you are in the choir, right?"

A young woman nodded with a shy smile.

"Ah—you must have been late like I was..." he said with a chuckle. "Now, are there any other choir members on this side of the door?"

A few hands went up. Dwight asked the choir members to climb onto the low roof of a nearby shed. The thousands gathered outside the hall fell silent as they realized they were about to have front-row seats to Dwight's sermon. Inside the hall, the singing had ceased as word spread like wildfire that Dwight was just outside and was preparing to speak. Dwight smiled as he imagined the intense relief on Ira's face and in his heart.

When the choir had assembled, Dwight asked them to sing a few songs. Thousands gushed from the building into the wide gardens and surrounded the carriage on which Dwight was perched. When everyone was settled and a comfortable hush had fallen over the sprawling crowd. Dwight stood up on the box to preach.

He spoke for nearly an hour, presenting the clear truths of salvation. The sun was setting, bathing everything in a golden glow. The gardens were lush and fragrant with springtime buds and blossoms. The effect was spellbinding, and Dwight's clear, strong voice rang out across the landscape.

As the sermon closed, Dwight asked those interested in salvation to enter the hall while the others adjourned to a nearby church to pray. Dwight climbed down from the carriage and entered the hall to find a sizeable crowd.

He mounted the platform and asked the crowd, "How many of you have not yet been saved but would like to be before you leave tonight?"

He had to blink back tears of joy as more than 2,000 people rose from their seats!

Not everyone was so easily won, however. In Northern Scotland, where Dwight traveled after Glasgow, an employer was converted during a service, and he decided he wanted each of his employees to experience the same joy he was feeling. One-by-one, he sent his employees to Dwight's meetings, and one-by-one, they found Jesus. But one employee steadfastly refused to attend a meeting, saying he would rather remain unsaved than be converted by an un-ordained American.

Despite his employer's persistent pleas, the employee never relented, and Dwight moved on to another town. Some weeks later, the employee was sent on business to the town of Inverness. When he had finished his work for the day, he decided to take a stroll by the river. As he walked by the water, the employee saw a large crowd gathered up ahead. Curious, he joined the crowd.

A man was preaching on a low platform. The employee could not quite see the preacher, but he could clearly hear his low, booming voice. As he listened to the message of God's love, the employee's heart was touched. He tearfully gave his heart and life to Christ's service. When the meeting was over, he asked some of the listeners for the name of the man who had been speaking. To his great surprise, it was Dwight L. Moody—the very man he had refused to go see!

After nearly a year in Scotland, Dwight trained a young man named Henry Drummond to carry on the work. Then he set himself to praying. Where would God have him go next?

Influencing Ireland

There had been nearly 5,000 conversions in Scotland as a direct result of Dwight's ministry, and that had caught the attention of the whole United Kingdom. Pastors in London pleaded with Dwight to come and minister there, but there was still a great deal of division and fighting among the London churches. Dwight did his best not to go to places where the churches were not united in the name of Christ. So, Dwight decided to go to Ireland instead.

The first Irish mission began in Belfast on September 6th, 1874. At 8:00 that morning, Christian workers met in Dugall's Square Chapel. It was a large building, but even at that early hour, it felt crowded. There were three services that day, each larger than the last, and by the final service of the day, they had moved to the largest church in town. But even that was not sufficient, as the auditorium was filled to its 2,000-seat capacity and hundreds more spilled into the streets.

Noon prayer meetings were soon established, and they became the foundation for the success of the mission. The prayer meetings routinely had an attendance of over 1,000 people, and the evening services were so large they had to be split into two separate meetings. There was a 2:00 p.m. service for the women, and an evening service for the men. God blessed this arrangement—the services continued to grow, and a mission spread to neighboring towns.

On October 8th, just a month after arriving in Belfast, Dwight held an open-air meeting that was one of the largest ever held in Ireland. At every meeting, Dwight presented the opportunity to become a Christian, and at every meeting, people responded. By his last service in Belfast, just six weeks after arriving in Ireland, over 2,100 people had been converted.

From Belfast, Dwight moved on to Dublin. The churches in Dublin came together to support Dwight and his ministry. Noon prayer meetings were established almost immediately, and evening services were held at the Exhibition Palace, the largest building in all of Dublin.

Thousands of people attended every service. Both Catholics and Protestants, who had fought bitterly for generations, were brought together by the Word of God. The love of God and the Word of God reached out to sinners from both backgrounds and brought them to salvation.

After his work in Dublin was done, Dwight headed back to England. He still felt the time was not right to go to London, so he visited several cities, speaking, ministering, and even raising funds for local YMCAs. Finally, he set his sights on Sheffield for the next big campaign.

The meetings in Sheffield began with a watch-night service on December 31st, 1874. In a later meeting, Dwight chided the Christians of Sheffield—and every other city—for their lack of passion to reach lost souls around them.

"I have been told," Dwight said, "that there are about 150,000 un-churched people in this city. And to make matters worse, there are no churches near them, even if they wanted to go."

He paused and surveyed the crowd, his eyes dark and flashing. "It seems to me that if there be upon God's earth one blacker sight than these thousands of Christless and graceless souls, it is the thousands of dead and slumbering Christians living in their very midst, rubbing shoulders with them every day upon the streets, and never so much as lifting up a little finger to warn them of death and eternity and judgment to come."

"I believe," he went on, "that if there is one thing which pierces the Master's heart with unutterable grief, it is not the world's iniquity, but the church's indifference."

After several weeks in Sheffield, Dwight and Ira moved on to Birmingham, England. They were only there for two weeks, but the effects of the ministry were astounding. Between 3,000 and 6,000 people met every morning for a half hour. In the afternoon, the forty-five-minute services also ran 3,000 to 6,000 in attendance. But the evenings were the most remarkable, with 13,000 to 15,000 attending every night. In fact, in the first eight days at Birmingham, more than 106,000 people came to hear Dwight preach.

From Birmingham, Dwight went on to Liverpool, where a special hall had to be built because no existing building could hold Dwight's audiences. Dubbed Victoria Hall, it was 174 feet long and 124 feet wide, and it seated 10,000 adults. For a children's service one Saturday, 12,000 children squeezed in to hear the story of the Wordless Book, with its black page for sin, its red page for the blood of Jesus, its white page for a cleansed heart, and its gold page for the beauty of Heaven.

Dwight also raised money for a YMCA hall in Liverpool. Once the funds were raised, however, Dwight called on his friend and assistant Henry Drummond to help with the project. Dwight had somewhere else he needed to be!

London at Last

It was finally time for Dwight to go to London, arguably the wickedest city in England. Just prior to Dwight's arrival in early 1875, statistics were published indicating more than a third of all crime in England was committed in London, and the city had approximately one million un-churched residents. Dwight's heart was burdened by these statistics, and he determined to make as much of a difference as he could on the famed city of London.

Before Dwight held any meetings in London, nearly 2,000 pastors and Christian workers gathered on February 8th, 1875 to question Dwight and find out if he was really the person he said he was. Dwight corrected many rumors at this meeting, including the idea that he was leading people astray in the inquiry rooms, the rumor that he was taking royalty money on the hymnals, and the absurdity that Moody and Sankey were not ministers at all but traveling organ salesmen.

"Will you be printing your creed prior to holding services here?" came one of the last questions.

"My creed, sir, is already printed."

"Where can we find it, Mr. Moody?"

Dwight grinned. "You'll find it in Isaiah 53."

"What will be your goal in these meetings?" another person posed. "Will it be primarily evangelism?"

"No," Dwight said. "Of course, I will present the gospel and help people find Jesus. But I intend the main goal of this campaign to be preaching to Christians. I would rather wake up a slumbering church than a slumbering world."

The first meeting in London was held on March 9th, and 17,000 people attended. Thousands more had to be turned away. As exciting as this turn out was, Dwight stressed those in attendance should focus on God and what He was doing instead of the excitement of the meetings. To facilitate the large number of attendees, however, Dwight separated the services into early ones for women and children and evening services for the men. This worked well, just as it had in Belfast.

Bow Road Hall was a building cobbled together for Dwight's meetings. In the heart of London's tough East End, it was made of corrugated iron, nearly an acre in size, with a sawdust floor and 9,000 cane-bottom chairs. The walls were red flannel, with Scriptures on them in white letters that were two feet tall. There were 100 young men and women in the choir, and on the night of the first meeting, the hall was filled to its 10,000-person capacity more than a half hour before the service was scheduled to start. Many hundreds were turned away, as there was not even a bit of standing space.

In sharp contrast to the rough-and-tumble crowd at Bow Road Hall, Dwight also held meetings in the fashionable West End, where noon prayer meetings and early evening meetings were held in the Royal Opera House. Other meetings were held at Camberwell Green Hall, where a special service was held for children from forty-seven different children's homes, orphanages, and schools for the blind and crippled. They came to hear Dwight's stories and Ira's singing and to have their questions about God and His Word answered.

During this series of meetings, Dwight would awaken early and have a personal devotion, spend time in prayer, and handle any correspondence or personal or business matters that needed his attention. By noon, he was at the Royal Opera House in the West End for a meeting. He then had lunch and read his Bible at 3:30 p.m., followed by an early meeting in the West End at 5:00 p.m. As soon as that meeting was over, Dwight would climb in a carriage for the five-mile drive to Bow Road Hall in the East End, where the services began at 8:00 p.m. After meeting and talking with all who were interested in salvation, Dwight would climb back in the carriage for the long ride back to his room. It was a busy schedule, but Dwight loved it.

In their last week in London, Dwight and Ira were invited to Eton College, an elite boys' school for 900 students near Windsor Palace. Dwight was excited about this invitation, but just before the meeting was to be held, a Member of Parliament named Mr. Knatch Bull-Hugessen started an opposition movement to the services. There was so much controversy over the meeting that it was even discussed in the British House of Lords!

Despite the opposition, Dwight saw no reason to change their plans. But when they arrived in Windsor just after noon on the day of the meeting, they were told they could not use the tent space they had been promised. They were also denied use of the town square. Finally, a generous citizen offered the use of his garden. Just after 3:00 p.m., a group of 200 boys from Eton arrived. By the start of the meeting, nearly 1,000 people were packed into the garden. Ira led singing, and Dwight offered a prayer. Then he stood on a small hill under a chestnut tree and spoke from his heart about the benefits of choosing early to live a Christian life.

In the course of his four-month mission in London, Dwight held 285 meetings and addressed more than 2.5 million people. Those numbers are mind-boggling, even by modern standards, but they were absolutely unthinkable during that time. Tired—but very happy to have been greatly used by God—Dwight and Ira and the Moody family left England on August 14th, 1875, after a little more than two years ministering in the United Kingdom. It was time to go home for some rest. But Dwight did not realize that his popularity overseas had compounded his popularity in the United States, and rest would be very hard to come by!

American Campaigns

After landing in New York, the Moody family traveled to Northfield, Massachusetts, Dwight's hometown, to have some rest and relaxation. Dwight found great joy in visiting his aging mother and other family members. In fact, he liked it so much that he purchased a twelve-acre piece of property in Northfield, near his old family home, and had a house built on it for his family. It became a frequent retreat for Dwight and a home for the family, far from the hustle and bustle of Chicago and the other big cities where Dwight often ministered.

As soon as Dwight arrived, invitations poured in. At first he rejected all of them in an attempt to rest. But his need to be busy got the best of him, and by early September, he had called together some close friends to help plan a schedule for a series of American campaigns in the winter of 1875 and early parts of 1876. Dwight also made time to hold two weeks of meetings at one of the old churches in Northfield, and nearly the whole town attended. People also traveled from many miles away to pack the auditorium.

111

For his winter campaigns, Dwight decided to focus on the big cities instead of the smaller towns.

"Water runs downhill," he told a close friend, "and the highest hills in America are the great cities. If we can stir them, we shall stir the whole country."

The first American campaign began in Brooklyn in October. Those meetings were quickly followed by a series of meetings in Philadelphia. The meetings in Philadelphia were held in the recently abandoned freight depot of the Pennsylvania Railroad. It was converted to seat 13,000, but the meetings were so popular that even that was not enough. Separate meetings were arranged early in the day and later in the evening to fully accommodate the crowds. On Sunday morning, people would start lining up at 4:30 a.m. for the 8:00 a.m. meeting. By 6:00 a.m., there was typically such a large crowd that they had to open the doors.

The last stop that winter was New York City, where Dwight spoke at the Hippodrome, on the site of what is now Madison Square Garden. The building was separated into two theaters, each holding 7,000 people. By seven o'clock on Sunday mornings, a crowd had already gathered for the eight o'clock meeting. People stood chatting pleasantly with each other. Some were even seen inviting street folks and others out in the early morning. The doors opened at 7:15 a.m., and the crowd would surge in. It was a strange and beautiful mix of races, classes, ages, and other features—a perfect picture of the way God's love and forgiveness overcome all human boundaries. At 7:40 a.m., the choir would begin to sing, and at 8:00 a.m., Moody and Sankey would take their places.

The meetings were remarkably successful. Many speculated that Dwight could relate to the masses because he was one of them, not elite or educated, as many preachers were. He had no polish, no evidence of prettiness or pampering. He was straightforward and direct, telling things the way he saw them, and reaching out to others to draw them in and, ultimately, to the Savior.

Dwight took the summer of 1876 off to spend with his family at Northfield. In the fall, he traveled to Chicago—the city dearest to his heart—for a special campaign. A tabernacle had been built for him with seating for 10,000. The campaign was wildly successful, and the churches throughout Chicago experienced great growth as a result of the conversions and rededications.

After one meeting, a minister came to him. "Tell me, Mr. Moody," he said, "how many people have been saved under your ministry?"

"I don't know anything about that, sir," Dwight replied. "Thank God, I don't have to. I don't keep the Lamb's Book of Life."

Each fall and winter, Dwight held campaigns in other cities. In 1878-79, he found himself in Baltimore, a new city for him. During one service of that campaign, a criminal had worked his way into the crowd. A police detective, Todd B. Hall, was tracking him, and knew he was in the hall. Out of respect, Detective Hall did not want to disrupt the service, so he stood at the back to wait until it was over. While standing and listening, God touched his heart, and he became a believer. He immediately went and told his Chief of Detectives back at the police station. Then he went home and told his wife about his experience, and she accepted Christ as well!

After Baltimore, in 1879-80, Dwight went to St. Louis. The following year, he spent time on the Pacific Coast, visiting a number of cities in Colorado and California, as well as other states. There was no end to his energy or his zeal. But he knew there was a project back home in Northfield that God needed him to do, and he knew he had to make it a priority.

A Dream Becomes Reality

For many years—decades, even—Dwight had felt the keen need of better education for the unfortunate of society, particularly the young ladies. One day in the early 1870s while driving with his brother near Northfield, Dwight looked over and saw a small cottage, set back from the road and far removed from all neighbors and human contact. In the doorway of the cottage sat a woman and her two daughters, braiding straw into hats to sell at a city market. Dwight later learned the father was paralyzed in an accident, but he was very educated, and he always encouraged his daughters in education and industry.

It was for girls like those that Dwight wanted to build his school. One afternoon in 1878, as summer was coming to a close, Dwight stood by the road on his property at Northfield, discussing the idea of a girls' school with a friend from Boston. As they talked, Dwight noticed a man walking by who owned sixteen acres of land adjoining Dwight's property. Dwight stopped him and asked if the land was for sale.

"I suppose so," the man said.

"And how much do you want for it?"

The man gave Dwight a price, and his heart leaped for joy. Immediately he pulled the man into his house, drew up the papers, and completed the sale. In one afternoon, Dwight had identified and purchased the land he would need for the girls' school. Over the next year, several other adjoining plots of land were purchased until the estate totaled 100 acres. Then, in the spring of 1879, ground was broken for a large hall for 100. Building for the school had officially begun.

With characteristic impatience, Dwight did not want to wait for the school to be finished before he brought students in. He made some modifications to his family home, and the Northfield Seminary for Young Women officially opened on November 3rd, 1879, with classes being held in Dwight's dining room and students lodging in a makeshift dormitory. And two of the first students were the hat-making girls from the remote cottage!

During a conference at the girls' school in September 1880, Dwight announced that money had been donated, and land had been purchased, and he would be establishing a boys' school within the year, calling it Mt. Hermon. Both schools were priced at about half of the actual cost, making education attainable to even the poorest members of society. The education was good, and the curriculum was solid, but the price was reasonable enough that few were unable to afford it, and for those, Mr. Moody would make exceptions.

In both schools, manual labor was not just encouraged, but required. The girls learned and practiced domestic tasks, like cooking, cleaning, laundry, etc. The boys did handiwork and grounds work around the campus. Physical exercise was regularly encouraged, and learning was year-round, with a home-like atmosphere that made students feel like part of a family. And in the cornerstone of each main school building was a copy of the Bible, cemented in to illustrate that Christ was the foundation of both schools.

Despite the home-like atmosphere, learning was rigorous, and expectations were high. Students would rise at 6:00 a.m. every day, and would soon enter into private devotions before breakfast. At 7:00 a.m., breakfast was served and rooms had to be tidied. Then classes were held from 7:40 a.m. to 11:50 a.m., followed by chapel and lunch. After lunch was a two-hour period for manual labor. When the work was over, students had an hour of study and some free time before evening devotions and dinner. The day ended with two-and-a-half hours of studying and another half hour of personal devotions. Lights out was strictly enforced at 10:00 p.m. By that time, most students were happy to get some sleep.

While these two schools became a distinct priority for Dwight, there was still much more to his ministry, and some of his work took him far from his family again.

Scattered Responsibilities

While Dwight recognized the need for his presence and help at Northfield, he also saw a need to do a follow-up trip to the United Kingdom to check on the work that had been started six years earlier. In 1881, Dwight headed back to England to meet with the workers he had left in the cities of his major campaigns. He began in Northern England at Newcastle-upon-Tyne, and then continued to Edinburgh and Glasgow. It brought back memories, but it also gave him new things to pray for.

Children's meetings were held in most cities on Saturday mornings, and Dwight loved to teach the children using object lessons or "illustrated sermons", as he called them. For example, when teaching the children about being the light of the world, Dwight brought and lit a candle. He had a helper put a bushel over the candle to demonstrate how it blocked the light. Then the children cheered when the bushel was removed. His innovative approach helped reach people that may have otherwise never known Christ.

Many people in many places wanted to have Dwight visit, and he received more invitations than he could accept in a lifetime. He prayed over each one and carefully sought God's will. As he decided on which invitations to accept, Dwight traveled back to Northfield to check in on the schools, which were still in their early stages. Finding everything satisfactory, Dwight accepted an invitation to hold a lengthy campaign in London.

The London campaign began in November and lasted until mid summer. Halls were built at eleven different sites to accommodate more people in more areas of the city. Each hall held 5,000 people. Dwight traveled among the halls, sometimes preaching four or five times a day, but never less than twice. During the eight months of the campaign, he spoke to 2 million different people. The impact on London society was felt for years.

Returning to America, Dwight was burdened by the need for what he called "gap men". He wanted to train workers to bridge the gap between the everyday man and the pastors and clergymen. Dwight decided to open a training institute in Chicago to do this work, training men and women to evangelize.

To correspond with the establishment of this new school, Dwight started a series of evangelistic meetings in Chicago on December 31st, 1886. Meetings were held in roller-skating rinks. Noontime prayer meetings were held in Farwell Hall. A tent was purchased for further meetings. For a few years, informal evangelistic training was implemented and then practiced in meetings and campaigns. In May 1889, Dwight hosted an intensive, short-term evangelistic training meeting at the Chicago Avenue Church—his old church. He expected about twenty participants, but 200 showed up!

It thrilled Dwight's heart to see others catching the passion for souls. In fall 1889, the Chicago Bible Institute was formed and officially opened. It could house up to 200 male and female students, and it adjoined the Chicago Avenue Church. Students were offered a two-year training course focusing on doctrine, exposition, and music. The mornings were packed with classes, and the afternoons and evenings were practical exercises in personal evangelism, with students going out and ministering firsthand to the people of Chicago, telling them about Christ.

Dwight was pleased with the schools God had given him to manage, and he traveled amongst the three, ensuring things were running smoothly and biblical principles were being consistently applied. He loved this work, and he didn't imagine he would ever again travel far from these special ministries. But Dwight had learned long before that when he made plans, God often changed them.

A Final British Adventure

In the early 1890s, as Dwight managed the three schools and a wealth of speaking engagements, a Scottish pastor visited Dwight at Northfield. Dwight welcomed him warmly.

"How are things there in Scotland, old friend?"

The Scottish pastor smiled. "Things are going well, but your presence is craved."

"I don't think I'll be making a trip like that again. I have far too much going on here. But the kind thoughts are greatly appreciated," Dwight said.

The pastor bent to open his travel bag. "Let me show you something."

He pulled out a huge roll of paper, nearly a foot in diameter. "This is a petition for you to come and visit us again. It comes from the people of more than fifty different towns and cities. Have a look…"

He unrolled the paper and it went through Dwight's sitting room, out the door, and across the yard. It was 150 feet long and contained more than 2,500 signatures of people begging Dwight to return and minister to them. His heart squeezed with compassion, and he knew he had to go one more time.

A few months later, Dwight arrived in the United Kingdom. He preached in more than 100 cities and towns, preaching three times each day in most places. People flocked to see him, and the results were miraculous. But Dwight was pushing hard—too hard, perhaps—and he got a cold that just kept getting worse. At one point he completely lost his voice. Finally, at the insistence of close friends, Dwight went to the doctor.

"Mr. Moody," the doctor said, "you most certainly have a bad cold. But did you also know you have a heart condition?"

Dwight shook his head. "No doctor has ever told me that before."

"Well, I'm telling you now, sir. Your heart is in trouble. You have to slow down and take it easy. You are literally killing yourself. You must learn to take it easy."

Dwight took this news and put it in a corner in his mind. He did not want to be a poor steward of his health, but taking it easy was not in his vocabulary. He did decide, however, that it was time for him to go home. Dwight and his son boarded the *Spree*, one of the fastest available ships, at Southampton. They were both looking forward to being home after such a long time away.

Three days into the voyage, as seasick Dwight lay on the couch in their room, an awful crashing noise reverberated through every deck of the ship. Dwight's son ran up to the main deck and came back breathless.

"The ship is sinking, Father," he said. "It is going down!"

Dwight got dressed and decided to investigate for himself. He went up to the top deck. Many of the other passengers were there, asking questions.

"It's just a broken shaft," a crew member assured the passengers. "There is no real danger. We will be fine."

"Lies!" a man cried, running onto the deck. His clothes were wet and disheveled. "Those are lies. My cabin is nearly full of water!" He looked frantically at the other passengers. "Do you hear me? We are sinking!"

Panic flashed across the faces of the passengers. Crew members quickly went and closed the bulkheads in the affected areas, bracing them with large beams. The sinking stopped for the most part, but the ship was powerless, adrift in the middle of the Atlantic Ocean.

All day Saturday, they drifted. All day Sunday, they drifted. On Sunday night, Dwight spoke with the captain.

"Captain, sir, might I hold a religious service in the ship's saloon tonight?"

The captain's answer was quick and sure, "Mr. Moody, I think that's a wonderful idea. Please do. And if I am able to be spared from the bridge, I'll be there myself."

The service was announced, and nearly every passenger came. The ship was askew in the water, with the bow riding high and the stern sinking low into the water, so Dwight wrapped his arms around a post. He read Psalm 91, paying special attention to verse 11, which read, "For He shall give His angels charge over thee, to keep thee in all thy ways." His desperate audience clung to every phrase of hope from God's Word.

Just a few hours after the service, around 3:00 a.m. on Monday morning, the distress signals were seen by a passing steamer. They were towed back to port in England. It took ten days to get back, but the 700 passengers on the *Spree* were not complaining. They were too happy to be alive!

After a brief rest at Northfield, Dwight traveled to Chicago to spend six months ministering to the vast multitudes who were flocking to the city for the 1893 World's Fair. Dwight coordinated ministries that would compete with the attraction of the World's Fair, employing special speakers and gifted singers, and purchasing plenty of advertising. Dwight rented nine large theater halls. Five large tents were in constant use. Two gospel wagons traveled the city, distributing tracts, and serving as a platform for street speaking and singing. A shop in the heart of the city was converted to a mission. At all of these places, Bible Institute students helped conduct afternoon and evening services. There was also a special squad that started working at 10:00 p.m. to handle any issues that might come up overnight.

In addition to these venues, the manager of Forepaugh's Circus agreed to rent Dwight the big tent for the two Sunday mornings they were in town. The tent seated 10,000, with standing room for 10,000 more. Many circus employees joked that Dwight would be lucky to get 3,000 people there. To their great surprise, 18,000 showed up the first Sunday, and even more came the second week.

Dwight's topic that first Sunday was, "The Son of Man Is Come to Seek and to Save That Which Was Lost". Toward the end of the sermon, a lost child was noticed and passed up to the platform. Dwight held her high so her parents could see and recognize her. A father soon came running.

"Does this little one belong to you?" Dwight asked, cradling the little girl.

"Yes. Thank you so much, Mr. Moody!"

Dwight handed the child to her father and said to the crowd, "That is what Jesus Christ came to do—to seek and save lost sinners and restore them to their Heavenly Father's embrace."

At the end of the service, people flooded the aisles to meet Christ. And by the end of the World's Fair, more than 125 services had been held, and thousands of lives had been touched and changed. Dwight was exhausted, and he was growing weaker, but he still had a few more things to do.

The Final Chapter

In the years following the World's Fair, Dwight's pace slowed, but he kept going. In the fall of 1895, he spoke for several weeks at the Atlanta Exposition, drawing crowds of thousands for each service. In early 1897, Dwight held a campaign in Boston, speaking twice a day every day except Saturday. One night after a service at Tremont Temple in Boston, a well-dressed young man approached Dwight.

"Mr. Moody, I am leaving for California tomorrow, but I had to speak to you."

"What is it, young man?" Dwight asked.

"Twenty-five years ago, you were speaking in London," the young man told him. "I was there with two friends, and we were very evil boys. We were always in trouble. But that night, as we heard you speak, we each made a decision to give our lives to Jesus. As we came out of the service, we all shook hands and promised each other that we would start a new life."

"And did you all keep that promise?" Dwight asked.

"Oh yes, sir," the young man said. "Here I am, of course. One of the others died leading a military regiment in Egypt. And the third is a missionary in Africa. Mr. Moody, you changed our lives."

"No, God changed your lives," Dwight corrected. "But I am pleased to have been His instrument."

While in Boston, Dwight was interviewed by a newspaper reporter.

"What was the principal event for good in your life?" the reporter asked.

"Well, a good many events have been for good," Dwight answered, "but perhaps none better than the surrender of my will to God."

"And what advice would you give, Mr. Moody, to young men?"

Dwight thought for a moment. "Seek first the Kingdom of God and His righteousness, and all these things shall be added unto you."

In late 1899, despite declining health, Dwight assured Emma that he was well enough to travel to Kansas City to conduct a series of meetings. But at the breakfast table on a crisp November morning, the choir conductor for the meetings noticed Dwight looked quite pale.

"Did you sleep well last night, Dwight?"

Dwight sighed and shook his head. "I had to sleep upright in my chair all night."

"What is the matter? Why did you need to do that?"

"I have had a pain in my chest for the past few weeks," Dwight admitted. "I did not let my family know it, for they would not have let me come here."

The choir conductor finally convinced Dwight to call the doctor, who administered some medicine. Dwight said he was feeling better. He continued on, preaching six more sermons. During the sermons, his voice was strong, his eyes flashing, his gestures vigorous. But afterward, he was growing weaker and weaker. Often, he needed a carriage to get to and from the meeting hall, even though it was only two short blocks from his room.

Dwight did not tell his family of his troubles until the day he was headed home. On November 17th, the doctor finally convinced him to stop working and leave Kansas City on the evening train. As they traveled, however, the train was delayed due to mechanical difficulties, and Dwight was afraid he would miss his connections.

At Detroit, a new engineer came on board. He heard Dwight Moody was on board his train and his demeanor changed.

"Send a message to Mr. Moody for me," he told the conductor. "Tell him I will do everything I can to get him where he needs to be on time. I was converted under his preaching fifteen years ago, and I owe him everything."

True to his word, the engineer got Dwight to the next stop on time. When he finally arrived at

Northfield, his family drove him home from the station. He insisted he was feeling better and went upstairs to prepare for tea, but when he was done, he was too weak to come back down the stairs. He spent his last weeks in his bedroom, surrounded by family. They read to him, talked with him, and simply sat with him. He grew weaker every day, but he was always smiling and cheerful.

On December 21ˢᵗ, he seemed a bit nervous.

"Are you comfortable?" his wife, Emma asked.

"Oh yes! God is very good to me—and so is my family."

Around 7:00 a.m. on December 22ⁿᵈ, Dwight began speaking in a low voice. His son was sitting beside him and leaned in closely to hear what Dwight was saying.

"Earth recedes; Heaven opens before me," Dwight murmured. "This is no dream…it is beautiful. It is like a trance. If this is death, it is sweet. There is no valley here. God is calling me, and I must go."

Dwight closed his eyes on earth and opened them in Heaven, in the presence of the Savior he had loved so dearly and served so well.

Although the legendary figure was gone, the legacy lived on. The schools at Northfield and Mt. Hermon continued to thrive and grow. The Chicago Bible Institute was renamed Moody Bible Institute, and more than 100 years later, graduates still emerge from that school ready to serve their Lord. Few men have served

God more thoroughly, and few men in history have ever had a greater impact for the cause of Christ than His humble servant, Dwight Lyman Moody.

Bibliography

Chicago Historical Society. "The Great Chicago Fire." www.chicagohs.org. Accessed February 3rd, 2015.

Jackson, Dave and Neta. *Danger on the Flying Trapeze*. Minneapolis: Bethany House Publishers, 1995.

Lee, Albert. "Example That Encourages." *Our Daily Bread*. August 12th, 2014.

Moody, William R. *The Life of Dwight L. Moody*. (From the Official Authorized Edition [1900 Version]) Harrington, DE: Delmarva Publications, 2013.

Wiersbe, Warren. *50 People Every Christian Should Know*. Grand Rapids, MI: Baker Books, 2009.

D.L. Moody Timeline

1837	Dwight Lyman Moody is born in Northfield, Massachusetts.
1841	Dwight's father dies suddenly, leaving the family in great poverty.
1843	The Oregon Trail is established, and American families move westward.
1847-54	Dwight works odd jobs in nearby towns from age 10 to 17.
1848	The California Gold rush begins.
1854	Dwight moves to Boston and gets a job in his Uncle Samuel's shoe store.
1855	Sunday School teacher, Edward Kimball, leads Dwight to the Lord.
1856	Dwight moves to Chicago and gets a job selling shoes.
1858	Dwight starts the North Market Hall Sunday School, which will eventually become the Illinois Street Church.
1860	Presidential Candidate, Abraham Lincoln, visits the North Market Hall Sunday School and commends Dwight on his success.
1861	The Civil War begins.
1862	Dwight marries Emma Revell in Chicago.
1862-65	Camp Douglas is the site of many ministry campaigns.
1863	The Emancipation Proclamation is signed.
1867	Dwight goes on his first trip to minister in the United Kingdom.
1870	Dwight Moody and Ira Sankey become a team.
1871	The Great Chicago Fire rages for two days and destroys much of the city.
1872	Yellowstone National Park becomes the first National Park in the United States.

1873-75	Dwight and Ira hold a two-year campaign in the United Kingdom, ministering to well over three million people.
1875-79	Dwight holds campaigns in large American cities, including Brooklyn, Philadelphia, New York, Baltimore and Boston.
1876	Alexander Graham Bell invents the telephone.
1876	Dwight buys property in Northfield, Massachusetts for a family home and for two schools – one for girls and one for boys.
1879	Northfield Seminary for Young Women is established.
1881	Mt. Hermon School for Boys is established.
1881-84	Dwight travels to the United Kingdom for another campaign.
1882	The first Christmas tree with electric lights is created by Edward Johnson, an employee of Thomas Edison.
1884-86	Dwight holds campaigns in smaller American cities, trying to reach those with populations between 10,000 and 200,000.
1889	Chicago Bible Institute is established to train workers in practical evangelism and church work.
1891	Carnegie Hall opens in New York City.
1892	Dwight and his son nearly sink in the Atlantic Ocean while returning from another two-year campaign in the United Kingdom.
1893	Dwight holds campaigns at the World's Fair in Chicago.
1895	Dwight speaks for several weeks at the Atlanta Exposition.
1897	Dwight holds campaigns at Tremont Temple in Boston.
1898	The United States declares war on Spain.
1899	Dwight holds his last series of campaigns in Kansas City.
1899	Dwight dies at home in Northfield, Massachusetts at the age of 62.

Thinking Further Topics

Chapter 1: The First Decade
Dwight had many problems and challenges in his early life. Read Job 23:10. What does this verse say about hard times? Do you think God had a plan for Dwight's life? Does He have a plan for your life? How do you know?

Chapter 2: The Journey to Independence
Romans 10:13 says, "For whosoever shall call upon the name of the Lord shall be saved." How does this verse apply to Dwight's experience in the shoe store with his Sunday School teacher, Mr. Kimball? Is there anyone God cannot save? Explain your answer.

Chapter 3: A Western Adventure
Read Psalm 139:7-10. What do these verses say about God's presence? What evidence is there that God's presence followed Dwight from Boston to Chicago? What evidence do you have that God's presence is with you?

Chapter 4: Perspective Changes Everything
Dwight's life was forever changed by the dedication of the dying teacher. What specific things did the teacher do to honor God? Why do you think this experience had such an impact on Dwight? Have you ever experienced

anything that made you want to serve God more? If so, tell about your experience.

Chapter 5: A Full-time Focus
John 15:12 says, "This is my commandment, that you love one another, as I have loved you." How was Dwight's love for others demonstrated in his ministry? How can you demonstrate love for the people in your life?

Chapter 6: A World at War
During the Civil War, Dwight went wherever he was needed and wherever he could minister to lost souls. How is this an illustration of the command in Ecclesiastes 9:10? How can you live out this commandment in your life?

Chapter 7: Daily Dedication
Read Matthew 5:14-16. How did Dwight's life illustrate this? Does your life shine for God? How can you be a light for God in your life? Name three specific things you can do to shine God's light and bring glory to Him.

Chapter 8: One Devoted Man
During his first trip to England, Dwight heard a pastor say, "The world has yet to see what God can do with and for and through and in and by the man who is fully and wholly consecrated to Him." What do you think

this means? Why did it have such an impact on Dwight's life and ministry?

Chapter 9: Moorehouse's Messages
Henry Moorehouse and Dwight originally had very different views on God's attitude toward sinners. What do you think—does God feel mostly love or mostly judgment toward sinners? Support your view with a verse (or verses) from the Bible.

Chapter 10: Moody and Sankey
Amos 3:3 says, "Can two walk together, except they be agreed?" Moody and Sankey were a very powerful team. Why do you think that was true? How does Amos 3:3 relate to the partnership of Dwight and Ira? Do you have friends who share your faith? Why or why not?

Chapter 11: The Great Chicago Fire
The night the Great Chicago Fire began, Dwight encouraged the congregation to think about salvation for a week before making a choice for Christ. Was this a good idea or a bad idea? Why do you think Dwight made that decision? Read John 9:4. How does this verse relate to the urgency of salvation?

Chapter 12: Abroad Again
Read Acts 1:7-8. How did Dwight make these verses a reality? How can you live these verses in your life? What

do you think would happen if all believers were committed to being witnesses for Christ around the world?

Chapter 13: English Adventures
In one meeting, Dwight met a lady who felt she could not be saved—and couldn't even pray—because of a past sin in her life. How does sin affect us? What should we do about it? What does 1 John 1:9 say? In this verse, what is God promising to do?

Chapter 14: Saving Scotland
1 John 4:4 says, "Ye are of God, little children, and have overcome them: because greater is He that is in you, than he that is in the world." When Dwight's character and reputation were attacked, how did he overcome the lies? How did this verse apply to that situation? Have you seen this verse work in your life? If so, tell about your experience.

Chapter 15: God's Work in Glasgow
In Jeremiah 33:3, God promises to show us incredible things when we call on Him. What are some of the incredible things Dwight witnessed in his ministry? What incredible things have you seen God do in your life?

Chapter 16: Influencing Ireland
The task of sharing God's Word probably overwhelmed Dwight sometimes. How do you think Dwight

overcame obstacles of fear and tiredness? Read Philippians 4:13. Do you think this verse was true for Dwight? Is it true for you? Explain your answers.

Chapter 17: London at Last
Read 2 Corinthians 5:17. When we give our lives to Christ, what does this verse say happens to us? How was this verse proven true in Dwight's ministry? Can you think of specific ways people are changed when they accept Jesus as Lord?

Chapter 18: American Campaigns
John 12:32 says, "And I, if I be lifted up from the earth, will draw all men unto me." Think about Dwight's popularity and the size of the crowds that came to hear him. Do you think his popularity came from his gifts or abilities? Why or why not? How does God use people to draw the world to Him?

Chapter 19: A Dream Becomes Reality
Read Mark 10:13-16. How did Jesus feel about children? Do you think this was part of Dwight's motivation for establishing the Northfield and Mt. Hermon schools? What other factors caused Dwight to build schools for boys and girls?

Chapter 20: Scattered Responsibilities
In his many travels, Dwight saw a need for Bible teachers and church workers who were well educated

and knowledgeable about God's Word. What did he do to help solve this problem? Do you think this was a good solution? Can you think of any verses that encourage believers to learn more about God and His Word?

Chapter 21: A Final British Adventure

In Galatians 6:9, believers are encouraged to work hard for God, and not to get discouraged or weary. As he got older, Dwight probably found traveling and ministering more difficult. How did his life follow the verse from Galatians? What reward did he see for his efforts? Can you think of some practical ways to apply this verse in your life?

Chapter 22: The Final Chapter

Read Matthew 25:23. Hearing God say, "Well done, thou good and faithful servant," should be the goal of every believer. Do you think Dwight lived a life worthy of this praise from God? Why or why not? How are you living your life? Do you think your life makes God pleased? If not, what changes do you need to make?

Author's Notes

All my life, I have heard pastors speak about the impact of D.L. Moody's ministry on modern Christianity. I knew of him more as a religious icon than as an actual person—a near-mythical figure that embodied the very spirit of evangelism. But my research for this book opened my eyes to the man behind the myth, and my heart was moved by what I saw.

As I read nineteenth century books by Dwight Moody's son and co-workers, as well as later works written about Dwight's life, I saw a very real man who did really amazing things for God. As I read the sermons and letters he wrote, I glimpsed his passion, his vision, and his desperate love for His Lord and lost souls. He grew beyond the legend and legacy I had always known and became a son, a brother, a husband, a father, and a friend.

D.L. Moody was fiery and fun, courageous and compassionate, hardworking and humble. His son once described him as, "A stout and bearded Peter Pan—a boy who never really grew up." He was the kind of man who could just as easily address a crowd of 20,000 on the Scottish hillsides or a prayer group of half a dozen in a church vestibule. He could give Abraham Lincoln a tour of his Sunday School facilities in the morning, and then spend the afternoon leading a pony through the Chicago streets to draw children to church. He was willing to go anywhere and do anything that was necessary to further the cause of Christ.

When I think of the D.L. Moody that I have come to know, I cannot help but think of a verse spoken by John the Baptist about Jesus. It is found in John 3:30, and it says, "He must increase, but I must decrease." Dwight was consistently pointing people toward Jesus. He could have used his fame to make a fortune or gain a following for himself. But he didn't. It was all about the Father, all about God increasing and Dwight decreasing.

Dwight Moody was remarkable, faithful, committed, and tireless. His life has become an inspiration to me. I hope people will see in my life the world-changing love and dedication I saw in his life. And I hope that every reader will see the real difference that one devoted person can make for God.

Trailblazer Series

There are over 40 different titles in the Trailblazer Series. To find out more about these amazing Christian lives, go to www.christianfocus.com.